GOD'S PRESCRIPTION FOR ✚ A HEALTHY CHRISTIAN

James Merritt

VICTOR BOOKS®

A DIVISION OF SCRIPTURE PRESS PUBLICATIONS INC.
USA CANADA ENGLAND

Unless otherwise noted, Scripture quotations are from *The Holy Bible, New King James Version.* © 1979, 1980, 1982 by Thomas Nelson, Inc., Nashville, Tennessee. Other quotations are taken from the *Authorized (King James) Version* (KJV).

Library of Congress Cataloging-in-Publication Data

Merritt, James Gregory, 1952 –
    God's prescription for a healthy Christian / by James Merritt.
      p.   cm.
    ISBN 0-89693-539-6
    1. Christian life – Biblical teaching. 2. Bible. N.T.
Corinthians, 1st – Criticism, interpretation, etc. I. Title.
BS2675.6.C48M47 1990
248.4 – dc20   90-39933
                                          CIP

1 2 3 4 5 6 7 8 9 10 Printing/Year 94 93 92 91 90

GOD'S PRESCRIPTION FOR ✚ A HEALTHY CHRISTIAN

———

CONTENTS

INTRODUCTION

One does not have to read the Book of 1 Corinthians very long to realize that it was written to a sick church in the middle of a sinful city. You would have had no trouble living the hard life in the fast lane in this ancient city. Corinth was a *luxurious* city located on the coast of the Mediterranean Sea. It was a vacation resort. It was a favorite gathering place of the playboys of that day. Pleasure palaces and entertainment centers abounded, affording all of the entertainment that one could enjoy in that day.

Corinth was a *lively* city. It was a strategic seaport and ships and people from all over the world came to the city. It had a beautiful gleaming stadium where the Isthmian games were held. It was a social, economical, and intellectual capital where some of the finest architecture in the world could be viewed.

Corinth was a *lascivious* city. On top of a 2,000-foot granite mount stood an acropolis, a temple of pagan worship. The goddess of this city was Aphrodite, the goddess of love. Night after night, up to 1,000 religious prostitutes would fill the streets looking to ply their trade. In short, Corinth could hold its own with any major city in the world today.

Sitting in the middle of this sinful city was a sick church. There are several reasons why this church at Corinth was spiritually sick. First of all, it was a *defiled* church. There was sin in the sanctuary, and there was sin in the Sunday School. One man was living in adultery with his stepmother, flaunting his immorality before the church, while the church stood by doing nothing about it. The members of the church were getting drunk during the taking of the Lord's Supper. The church was full of former homosexuals, adulterers, and fornicators struggling in their new life with God.

But it was also a *divided* church. This church was at civil war, and the war wasn't too civil! There were so many lawsuits going on between the members of the church that Perry Mason had been asked to serve as chairman of the deacons! Whenever you saw a church member coming down the street you would be just as likely to say, "I'll see you in court" as you would be to say, "I'll see you in church."

Furthermore, it was a *disgraced* church. It was the laughing stock of the city. The work of the church had been paralyzed. The worship of the church had been demoralized. And the witness of the church had been compromised.

A sick church is nothing more than a church filled with sick Christians. This church needed a fresh touch from the Great Physician who has the power to heal not only physical, but also spiritual sickness. I believe Paul wrote his Corinthian letter as a "prescription for healthy Christianity." Though the book was written to the church, I believe its main application is to the individual Christian.

If you believe that your own Christian walk is slightly anemic, a little bit weak, or struggling to maintain its vitality, I encourage you to read on and find *God's prescription for a healthy Christian.*

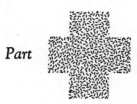

Part THE **One**

WORTH

OF A

HEALTHY

CHRISTIAN

•

THE OLD RUGGED CROSS

For over 2,000 years the sign and symbol of the Christian faith has been an old rugged cross. It is amazing how many of our songs and hymns revolve around the subject of the Cross. One such song, of course, is "The Old Rugged Cross." But just think of some of the others that we sing almost week after week: "Lift High the Cross," "At Calvary," "Am I a Soldier of the Cross?" "Down at the Cross Where My Saviour Died," "When I Survey the Wondrous Cross," "Beneath the Cross of Jesus," "At the Cross," "Were You There When They Crucified My Lord?"

The Cross is very special to those of us who love the Lord Jesus Christ. But we must remember that it is not so much the cross that we honor, as it is the One who died on it. We do not exalt those cross beams; those rugged blood-soaked pieces of timber that stood on Golgotha centuries ago. It is because of the One who hung on it that we honor it so very much.

We should honor it. We are to remember what took place on that cross 2,000 years ago. It is amazing to me to think that Jesus never asked us to remember His birth. Jesus never asked us to remember His resurrection. But when He instituted the Lord's Supper, He told us to remember His death.

Paul makes an amazing statement in Galatians 6:14. Paul said that he was going to glory in the Cross of the Lord Jesus Christ.

Now can you imagine someone finding glory in the electric chair, or glory in the gallows? Yet Paul said he was going to glory in the Cross! You will understand why Paul gloried, reveled, and marveled at the Cross when you see just what the old rugged cross really means to you and to me.

THE POWER OF THE CROSS IN SALVATION

It is in the Cross that the power of salvation comes forth. Paul speaks of the message of the Cross being the power of God in 1 Corinthians 1:18. The word *message* literally should be translated "word." The word of the Cross is the power of God. Now this word is not what we say about the Cross, it is rather what the Cross says to us.

The word of the Cross is God's first and last word of salvation. It is God's first word because Jesus was slain before the foundation of this world. But it is also God's last word of salvation, for this is where God has finally and forever provided a way for one to be saved and to go to heaven. It is God's plan of salvation. If a person is going to be saved, he or she must come to the Cross of the Lord Jesus Christ.

It Is a Unique Plan

There is no "Plan B" to salvation. The only highway that goes to heaven goes right through Calvary. You can't bypass the Cross if you want to go to heaven. You cannot go around the Cross if you want eternal life. Hebrews 9:22 states "Without shedding of blood there is no remission."

This is why men hate the Cross so much. It leaves no room for human merit, human achievement, nor human work. It is all of grace. You may say, "I don't like the way of the Cross. I like my way better. I like the way of going to church and being baptized, living a good life, doing good, and earning my way into heaven. That is the way I like best." Scripture speaks to such an attitude. "There is a way which seems right to a man, but its end is the way of death" (Prov. 14:12). The Cross is not the best way to heaven, the Cross is the only way to heaven.

I was watching a talk show not long ago and one of the Christian television personalities was asked the question, "Is a Jew, without Jesus Christ, lost?" I was disappointed with his answer because the man, who is a leading spokesman of the Christian faith, waffled this way and waffled that way, and finally said, "The Jews have their way of going to heaven and the Christians have their way of going to heaven."

But the Cross is not your way of going to heaven or my way of going to heaven; it is God's way of going to heaven. Not only is a Jew lost without Jesus, a Gentile is lost without Jesus. One of my own children, my own mother, without Jesus Christ, would be lost. If you are going to go to heaven, you are going to have to go the way of the Cross. It is God's unique plan.

> I must needs go home
>> By the way of the Cross,
> There's no other way but this.
>> I shall ne'er get sight
> Of the Gates of Light,
>> If the way of the ross I miss.

Jessie B. Pound's words ring clear. For only "the way of the Cross leads home." It is God's unique plan.

It Is a Universal Plan

Paul says that the Cross and Christ crucified is the power of God, both to the Jews and to the Greeks (1 Cor. 1:23). The Bible divides the world into two basic groups. Spiritually, the Bible says, there are the wheat and there are the tares. There are sheep and there are goats.

But nationally and ethnically the Bible says there are Jews and Greeks. Or, there are Jews and Gentiles. You are either a Jew or a Gentile. It doesn't matter what color you are, what language you speak, or what country you were born in; you are either a Jew or a Gentile. Now when Scripture speaks of Jews and Greeks, it is simply the biblical way of speaking of everybody.

The Cross is not the Gentile way to be saved, or the Western way to be saved, or even the Baptist way to be saved; the Cross is everybody's way to be saved.

God did not so love the Baptist, or love the West, or love America; God so loved this world that He gave His only Son to die on an old rugged cross (John 3:16). That is why Paul says in 1 Corinthians 1:24 that Jesus is both the power and the wisdom of God.

Think about it, all people have the same universal need. People need to *know* what is right and they need to *do* what is right. They need the wisdom to know what to do, and then they need the power to do it. Christ, Paul says, offers both. In other words, Jesus is all that you need. Jesus is all the Gentile needs. Jesus is all the world really needs. The Cross is God's universal plan.

It Is an Unchangeable Plan

Paul, almost stubbornly, said he was going to preach Christ crucified. Now that is very interesting. Why wasn't he going to preach Christ incarnate, Christ virgin-born? Why not say, I preach Christ risen? There are three things that separate Jesus Christ from every other man who has ever lived—the cradle, the Cross, and the crown: His virgin birth, His substitutionary death, and His resurrection from the dead.

Without the cradle the Cross is *useless*. If Jesus had not been born of a virgin, He could not have taken my sins upon Himself because He would have had sin within Him. But without the crown, the Cross is *meaningless*. Because if Jesus had not been raised from the dead, it would have been proof positive that He was a liar and not the Lord, not the Son of God. But without the Cross, both the crown and the cradle are *needless*.

In the cradle Jesus was born the Son of God. At the tomb Jesus was raised King of kings. But it was at the Cross that Jesus became the Saviour of the world. I not only need a risen Lord, I need a crucified Saviour. It is Christ crucified, not Christ in the cradle, not Christ in the tomb, not Christ in the marketplace who saves; it is the Christ on the Cross that is the power of God to all who are being saved.

That is why the preaching of the Cross and preaching Christ crucified must be an absolute priority. We are told in 1 Corinthians 1:21 that it pleases God to save those who believe through the foolishness of preaching. Now, it is not foolish preaching that pleases God; there is enough foolish preaching going around. But it is the foolishness of the message being preached. It is the foolishness of preaching a crucified Saviour that God uses to save men and women.

I admire the Apostle Paul. He could have easily compromised the message. Paul could have said that the message of the Cross is a stumbling block to the Jews and it is foolishness to the Greek, so one should alter it, change it, make it more acceptable, tone it down, and polish it so that people will listen. But Paul knew that it was an unchangeable message because only in Christ crucified do we have Jesus Christ, the power and wisdom of God.

I believe that any preacher worth his salt had better be a preacher of the Cross. Someone once said to Charles Haddon Spurgeon, "All of your sermons sound exactly the same. Why is that?" Spurgeon responded, "Because I just take a text, anywhere in the Bible, and then make a beeline straight to the Cross."

Now I'm not saying that the Cross is all that we should preach, and neither did Paul. But the foundation and the center of all our preaching should be Christ crucified.

Billy Graham tells of a time early in his ministry. After preaching one night to a great crowd in the Cotton Bowl in Dallas, Texas, there was very little response to his message. As he was leaving the platform an old man came up to him, put his arm around him and said, "Billy, you didn't preach the Cross tonight. Your message was good, but you didn't preach the Cross."

That great evangelist went to his room, wept, and made a resolve. He said, "Oh God, so help me, there will never be a sermon that I preach again unless the Cross is central." God has used that evangelist to preach to more people and to see more people saved than any other preacher in the history of the

Christian faith. There is power indeed, wonder-working power in the Cross of salvation.

THE PURPOSE OF THE CROSS IN SEPARATION

The Cross not only saves some, it separates all. The Cross is the great divide. People don't mind religion; they don't mind the church. They don't really mind the Bible. But if you want to divide a group of people, you lay down the Cross and watch people scurry to one side or the other.

Paul speaks in 1 Corinthians 1:18 of those who are perishing and those who are being saved. Some people look upon the Cross as foolishness, but others look upon it as the power of God.

Now there are some who are perishing. The word perishing literally means "to be cut loose." There are some people who come to the Cross, are repelled by it, and then drift away from God. Then there are others who come to the Cross and are drawn by it. They come into fellowship with God.

The way you see the Cross determines whether or not you are perishing, or being saved. It is your response to the Cross that determines whether you are lost or saved, whether you are headed for hell or heaven. There are three different attitudes that one can take toward the Cross.

For some the Cross is a *stumbling block*. For some the Cross is *foolishness*. But for others the Cross is the *power of God*. Now to the Jews, the Cross was a stumbling block. We get the word *scandal* from that Greek word. The Cross was a scandal to the Jews. It was repulsive to them. It was disgusting to speak of a crucified Saviour. Then to the Greeks it was foolishness." To the Greeks the Cross was moronic; it was a joke. Yet to others still, it was indeed the power of God unto salvation.

Some Rejected the Cross

The Jews required a sign. They were looking for wonders. The Jews were looking for a political Messiah. They were searching for someone who would come storming up on a white charger, sword drawn, ready to restore the lost glory and kingdom of Israel as it was in the days of David and Solomon.

As they studied the Old Testament they read all about the coming kingdom, and they were looking for a Messiah who would come and set up an earthly throne and kingdom. Even the disciples, after the resurrection of Jesus, asked Him, "Lord, will You at this time restore the kingdom to Israel?" (Acts 1:6) The Jews were continuously looking for signs, wonders, and miracles of the coming Messiah.

Over and over Jesus spoke to these Jews about their need for a sign. He said, "Unless you people see signs and wonders, you will by no means believe" (John 4:48). He said again, "This is an evil generation. It seeks a sign, and no sign will be given to it except the sign of Jonah the Prophet" (Luke 11:29). Jesus said that this was to be the only sign. Now what did that mean?

Just as Jonah was in the belly of the sea monster three days and three nights, Jesus' sign was to be the crucified Saviour on a cross, in a tomb for three days and then raised from the dead.

God gave the Jews a sign, the sign of the Cross. It was the only sign they ever needed to be saved, yet instead of rejoicing they stumbled over it. Have you ever been looking for something, only to find that all the time it was just beneath your feet? So it was for the Jews with their stumbling block. It was just what they were looking for all the time, and yet they rejected it.

I once read the story of a man whose house was flooded. In fact, he was in the middle of the flood. So he got up on top of his roof and he said, "God, I want You to deliver me from this flood. I'm just going to trust You to do it."

Soon someone came by in a rowboat and offered to take the stranded man to safety. He said, "Oh no, that's all right. Don't worry about me. God will take care of me."

The flood waters kept coming up and up until they were almost at his waist. About that time a helicopter flew overhead and the man inside it said, "Take hold of the rope and climb up." The man responded, "Oh no, don't worry about me. God will take care of me and deliver me." The helicopter left and soon after that the flood waters rose, and the man drowned.

The next scene was in heaven. The man, still wet, walked up to the throne room of God and said, "I don't understand it, God. I asked You to deliver me and You let me drown. Why didn't You save me?" The Lord responded, "I sent you a rowboat and a helicopter. What else did you want?" He has done the same for us. God sent a sign, the sign of the Cross. What more could anyone want?

Some Ridiculed the Cross

To some the Cross is a stumbling block, but to others the Cross is a laughingstock. Some people reject the Cross, but others just ridicule it.

The Jews sought after wonders, but the Greeks sought after wisdom. The Greeks were known for their great philosophers and their knowledge. They had come to the point where they literally deified wisdom. They were worshiping at the shrine of science and knowledge. Does that sound familiar today in the twentieth century?

We have people today who say, "If you can't put it into the test tube or in a mathematical equation, we will not believe it." But you can't put the Cross in a crucible, and you can't put faith in a formula. The great philosopher, Pascal, said, "The heart has its reasons that reason knows nothing of."

The Greeks could not rationalize the fact of God coming down in a human body and dying on a cross. Their approach was, "If we can't understand it we will not accept it." Anything they couldn't understand they just laughed off.

There are people like that every day in this world. They laugh at Jesus. They laugh at the Cross. They make fun of us Bible-believing Christians who dare to believe the Word of God, who witness, and share our faith. But the Cross is no laughing matter. A person can laugh his way into hell, but he can't laugh his way out. Remember the Scripture, "The fear of the Lord is the beginning of wisdom" (Ps. 111:10).

Heaven is full of wise *men*. Hell is full of wise *guys*. You see, God is too wise to let man come to know Him by his own wisdom. Man cannot solve his problems because he will not recognize their source, which is sin. Furthermore, he will not recognize the solution, which is salvation. God is so wise that He is not going to let man come to Him by his own wisdom.

As a matter of fact, we are told in 1 Corinthians 3:19 that "the wisdom of this world is foolishness with God." Think about it, a world full of wisdom is just a thimble full of foolishness to God. The Prophet Jeremiah said, "The wise men are ashamed. They are dismayed and taken. Behold they have rejected the Word of the Lord; so what wisdom do they have?" (Jer. 8:9)

I read about a young man who made a zero on an examination. He went in to see the professor and said, "I do not believe I deserve this grade." The professor looked at it and said, "I don't either, but it was the lowest grade I could give." I believe that is the way God feels about our wisdom. It doesn't even deserve a zero on His scale. A Ph.D. may be a Doctor of Philosophy to us, but he is just a phenomenal dud to God!

The things of God are hidden from the wise and the prudent, but they have been revealed unto babes (Matt. 11:25). If a person is going to come to God, he or she will have to come as a little child (Matt. 18:3).

Some Received the Cross

There is only one way you can understand the Cross. There is only one way you can receive the Cross, and that is in humility and in faith. I heard of a man who was touring Italy. His name was Dr. Evans. A friend said to him, "There is a blessing you will receive if you will go to thus and such a place and see a painting of the crucifixion of Jesus Christ."

Dr. Evans said, "What is it like?"

He said, "Never mind what it is like. I want you to see it. You need to see it, and promise me that you will."

Dr. Evans said, "I will."

He went to the village where this painting was, and he came to the chapel there. The caretaker asked the question, "You've come to see the painting, haven't you?"

He said, "Why, yes I have."

The caretaker responded, "Follow me, and come right this way."

Dr. Evans was not prepared for what he was about to see in the painting. He was looking for a beautiful masterpiece of art. There was Jesus painted on the Cross, very obviously being crucified. But it seemed as if it was all out of proportion. It didn't make sense. It didn't seem to be a work of art at all. It seemed somehow grotesque. It seemed somehow to be top-heavy.

Dr. Evans questioned, "I don't understand this painting."

The caretaker replied, "Come closer." He did.

The caretaker said, "Get lower." He did.

He said, "Come closer." "Get lower." "Come closer." "Get lower."

Finally, Dr. Evans said he found himself kneeling at the very foot of the cross. When he looked up he saw the perspective from which the painting had been made, and he realized it didn't make sense until you kneeled at the cross.

It is only when you lay aside your ambitions, crucify your prejudice, die to your intellectual approach, and humble your pride, that you can look up to the Cross and truly understand it.

But I am telling you that the purpose of the Cross is separation. It is either foolishness to you or it is the power of God. The Cross is in the middle and you are either on one side or the other. You are either on the hell side of the Cross looking toward heaven, or you are on the heaven side looking toward hell. The Cross either stands between you and heaven, or it stands between you and hell. That is the purpose of the Cross; to separate us one from the other.

THE PROCESS OF THE CROSS IN SANCTIFICATION

In 1 Corinthians 1:18 Paul says that the Cross is the power of God, not to those of us who are saved, but to those of us who are being saved, present tense, who are continuously being saved.

The Bible speaks of salvation in three tenses. The Bible says I have been saved. The Bible says I am being saved. And the Bible says I will be saved. I have been saved from the penalty of sin. When I accepted Christ into my heart and accepted His payment for my sin I was forgiven once and forever, saved now and forever, never again to be lost.

But I not only have been saved from the *penalty* of sin, I am being saved from the *power* of sin. Then, there will come a day when I will be saved from the *presence* of sin.

I have been saved from the penalty of sin; that is justification. I will be saved from the presence of sin; that is glorification. But at this very moment I am being saved from the power of sin; that is sanctification. That is what Paul deals with in verse 18.

Salvation, someone has said, is a crisis followed by a process. It is a decision followed by a dynamic. Our problem is that we sometimes tend to leave the Cross in the past. But the Cross should be a part of our everyday lives.

Three things still bother me even though I have been saved for almost thirty years. Sin still bothers me. Satan still bothers me. And self still bothers me. Those are the three great enemies of every Christian.

You are not only saved from the penalty of sin, you are being saved from the power of sin, the power of Satan, and the power of self. The Cross not only represents the power of God in my salvation, it represents the process of God in my sanctification. You see, I am to come to the Cross for pardon, but I am to get on the Cross for power.

I have heard people say, "I want to be a believer, but it is too difficult to live the Christian life." Friend, it is not difficult to live the Christian life; it is *impossible* to live the Christian life! The only way that you can live the Christian life is to let the power and the person of Christ live through you. Now how do you do that? You get crucified.

Paul gave this principle, "I have been crucified with Christ; it is no longer I who live, but Christ lives in me; and the life which I now live in the flesh I live by faith in the Son of God, who loved me and gave Himself for me" (Gal. 2:20). Now here is the process: Jesus died *for* me. I died *with* Him. When I die *to* me,

He lives *in* me. When He lives *in* me, I can live *for* Him.

We need to come to the Cross, not only for salvation, but for sanctification; not only for pardon, but also for power. We are to get on the Cross every day and die to self.

Paul said, "I die daily" (1 Cor. 15:31). For you see, it is when I die that I really live. If you say that's foolishness that just tells me you are perishing. Remember, it is impossible to live the Christian life, and you are not to live the life of faith for God; He wants to live His life through you.

> I can't.
> Well, He never said you could.
> He can.
> He always said He would.

The victorious Christian life occurs when you crucify self and allow His resurrection life and power to live in you. That is sanctification, the process by which we become more and more like Jesus, and daily experience victory in Jesus over sin, self, and Satan.

Aleksandr Solzhenitsyn is a great Christian. You may know that he was for many years a prisoner in Soviet concentration camps. Like other prisoners he worked in the fields. His days were a pattern of back-breaking labor and slow starvation.

One day, he literally gave up living. He felt no purpose in fighting on. He felt as if his life would make no ultimate difference. Laying his shovel down, he walked over to a bench and sat down. He knew the penalty for sitting down was death. He knew at any moment that a guard would order him to get up, and when he failed to respond the guard would probably take his own shovel and beat him to death, for he had seen it happen many times.

As he was sitting there waiting for death to surely come, his head down, he felt a presence over him. He thought it was the guard. Slowly, he lifted his eyes. Standing there was an old man with a wrinkled, utterly expressionless face. This man had been in the prison many years. He was hunched over from the back-breaking labor he was forced to do. They had never communicated even a word because they were not allowed to talk. But this old man took a stick and in the sand at Solzhenitsyn's feet he traced out the sign of the Cross.

As Solzhenitsyn stared at that sign his entire perspective shifted. He knew that even though he was only one man against the all-powerful Soviet Empire, in that moment he also knew that the hope of all mankind was represented by that simple cross. He realized that it truly represented the greatest power in the universe. He slowly got up, picked up the shovel, and went back to work under the sign of the Cross.

To be a healthy Christian you must rediscover the power of the Cross in salvation, the purpose of the Cross in separation, and the process of the Cross in sanctification. When you do this and apply it to your everyday world you will live the victorious Christian life.

GOD'S ALL-STARS

Imagine you are choosing a basketball team. You would most likely choose the tallest players. If you are choosing a track team, you would probably choose the fastest runners. And if you are choosing a beauty queen, you obviously would choose the prettiest contestant. Finally, if you are choosing a debate team, you would most likely choose the brightest candidate.

It is usually the best, brightest, and most beautiful who become "all-stars." So often we look at the all-stars of life and it makes us realize just how normal the rest of us really are. The fact of the matter is, by human standards very few of us will ever be all-stars. There is only one Miss America. There is only one most valuable player. There is only one President of the United States.

It is interesting that the kind of people that we would choose to be all-stars are exactly the opposite of the kind of people that God chooses to be all-stars. Now I am grateful for any all-star who loves the Lord Jesus. I'm grateful for the beauty queens, football players, movie stars, and the rich and the famous who love Jesus Christ. There are all-stars in almost every area of life who love Jesus.

But so often these people when invited to give their testimonies, because they are famous and well-known, become a source of discouragement rather than a source of encouragement. I am afraid that many women, for example, look at the beauty queen who loves the Lord and say, "I'm just an ordinary housewife. I could never be used like her." Or many of us men look at the athlete who gives a dynamic testimony and say, "I am not athletically gifted. God could never use me like He uses him." Or perhaps we look at the famous celebrity and deep down many of us say, "Well, I'm just an old country boy from the backroads of Mayberry. God could never use me like He uses him."

I've got some wonderful news for you. It is usually man's zero that is most likely to become God's hero. It is the man that the world would choose last that God loves to choose first.

You see, God has a very wonderful plan. God has taken what the world calls a foolish message. For we are told in 1 Corinthians 1:18 "that the message of the Cross is foolishness." God has combined this foolish message with what the world calls foolish messengers. We are told in 1 Corinthians 1:27 that "God has chosen the foolish things of the world." God takes the foolish message, combines it with foolish messengers and the result is glory to God, and God is in the business of bringing glory to Himself. You may have been voted "most likely to succeed." You may have been voted "best looking." You may have been Phi Beta Kappa, but you do not do God a favor by serving Him. God does you a favor by using you.

Paul here is discussing the mighty calling of a mighty God. Now this is not the call to salvation, but the call to service. Many people have the idea that God only calls preachers and missionaries, and the rest of us can do whatever we want to. But God has a calling for all of His children. Paul begins by saying, "You see your calling, brethren" (1 Cor. 1:26). God has a calling for every Christian outside of the church body.

He has called some to be lawyers, some to be nurses, some to be shoe salesmen, and some to be truck drivers. But God also has a calling for all of us inside the church. God has called some of you to teach, some to be outreach leaders, and some to sing in the choir. But the people that God calls, the people God uses and chooses, His all-stars, are common ordinary people. It is the nobodies of earth that are the somebodies in heaven. Paul shares with us three surprises concerning the calling of God.

GOD'S CALLING IS PECULIAR

"For you see your calling, brethren, that not many wise according to the flesh, not many mighty, not many noble, are called" (1 Cor. 1:26). God does not use and choose the people that we normally think that He would or should. Let's take a closer look at God's calling.

God's Calling Is Not According to Intelligence

When Paul uses the word "wise" he is not referring to spiritual wisdom, but intellectual wisdom. That is why he adds the phrase, "according to the flesh." It doesn't take a certain IQ to be mightily used by God. A person can be an intellectual genius, but a spiritual ignoramus. Likewise, a person can be intellectually slow, but be a spiritual giant for God.

It is all too easy to get intellectually big for your spiritual britches. A classic example is the humanist. Humanism says that reason is more important than revelation, that man's mind is more important than God's Word. It is interesting, yet sad to note, that some of the most brightest men who have ever lived were atheists and infidels. Voltaire, the thoughtful French philosopher, and Bob Ingersoll, one of those brilliant intellects of the nineteenth century, were men educated, erudite, and eloquent, yet they hated God. They were brilliant men, but brilliant fools, for only "the fool has said in his heart, there is no God" (Psalm 14:1).

Many of the so-called wise people of this world are not nearly as wise as we think they are, or as they think they are. I heard of little first-grader who had memorized the multiplication tables and he came home and he said to his mom and dad, "2 x 2 = 4." They were convinced they had a genius on their hands.

Like many proud parents they called all the neighborhood over to their house to hear their little boy recite his multiplication tables. The dad said, "All right Son, tell us what you know." The little boy reared back his head and said, "2 x 2 = 4." His mother and father were beaming and smiling at their little genius. Then right in the middle of their pride and joy the little boy asked, "Daddy, what's a 2?"

I believe in education. I believe we ought to get all the education that we can. A full heart is no excuse for an empty head, and we should love the Lord our God with all of our minds (Matt. 22:37). I certainly put no premium on ignorance. I heard of one Christian brother who said in his prayer, "Lord, I thank Thee that I am ignorant." Somebody else said, "He sure has a lot to be thankful for."

I believe every Christian ought to be a student. And I believe every preacher ought to be a scholar of the Word of God. Paul was not advocating some half-hearted, mediocre, lazy, anti-intellectual Christianity. We ought to love God with our minds. We should never quit studying and learning.

I heard of a preacher in Pennsylvania who had a reputation as an expert fox hunter. An old Quaker said to him one day, "If I were a fox, I could hide me where thee could not find me." The preacher said, "And where would that be?" The Quaker said, "In thy study."

We ought to study. We ought to read. We ought to exercise our intellectual abilities to the fullest. But wisdom, in and of itself, does not move God to choose anybody because the wisdom of man is just foolishness with God. It is not the person with the big head, it is the one with the big heart that God uses.

God's Calling Is Not According to Influence

Not many "mighty" are called. Here Paul refers to people of great means, people with power, prestige, and possessions. God can use both the millionaire and the movie star, but He's not able to use very many of them.

For some reason these kind of people usually see no need for God. It is amazing to see how God has blessed so many Americans and yet these very blessings have become the greatest obstacle to them knowing Him. The most difficult place I have ever been soul-winning is on the top of Lookout Mountain,

Tennessee. I am told that there are more millionaires per square mile on that little mountain than anywhere else in the world. While I was pastoring in Kentucky, we took a youth group on a mission trip to Lookout Mountain. We began to go from door to door, literally from mansion to mansion, giving out tracts and trying to share the Gospel.

I remember particularly one lady that we visited because she was typical of most of the people who lived on that mountain. We knocked at one palatial home, and she answered the door. We said, "We're here to talk to you about Jesus." She replied, "I don't need you to talk to me about Jesus. I am an Episcopalian," and slammed the door.

We turned around and started to leave and noticed the gardener out cutting the lawn. We walked over to him and while she stood at the window ranting, raving, and asking us to leave, one of our group quietly led that gardener to Jesus. Not many mighty are called.

God's Calling Is Not According to Importance

Paul says, not many "noble" are called. The word noble is made up of two Greek words that literally mean "well-bred" or "well-born." Paul refers here to royal bluebloods, human thoroughbreds, people of nobility and pedigree. He is referring here to the Kennedys, Vanderbilts, and Rockefellers. Now certainly, some of these kind of people can be used, but many, if not most of these people will not be used.

But one word in verse 26 is extremely important to notice; it is the word *many*. Three times Paul uses that word *many*. Now Paul did not say "any," he said "many." Lady Huntingdon was one of the richest ladies in England, a well-to-do socialite. She was won to Jesus by a British evangelist named Rolland Hill. When she would give her testimony, she would say, "I was saved by one letter; the letter M." People would wonder what she meant. Then she would say, "I am so glad that the Bible says, "Not *many* noble," rather than not any noble.

I thank God for the wise, noble, and mighty who love the Lord. I thank God for any athlete, movie star, or millionaire who will give his or her life to Christ. But God's work is going to be done primarily not through the superstar preachers, evangelists, or celebrities; God's work is going to be done through His ordinary everyday run-of-the-mill people.

GOD'S CALLING IS PARTICULAR

Paul says, "God has chosen the foolish things of the world to put to shame the wise, and God has chosen the weak things of the world to put to shame the things which are mighty; and the base things of the world and the things which are despised God has chosen, and the things which are not, to bring to nothing the things that are" (1 Cor. 1:27-28). By and large, the kind of people that God is able to use, fall into three categories: the foolish, feeble, and familiar.

God Calls the Foolish

The word "foolish" comes from the Greek word *moros*. From it comes our word "moron." Now this is literally what Paul says. "God has chosen the morons of this world to put to shame the wise." God calls morons to serve Him.

When I think about the foolish people that God uses, I cannot help but think about Billy Sunday, one of my heroes. Billy Sunday was one of the greatest evangelists who ever lived, but he was certainly no brilliant intellectual. He was not highly educated. He would sometimes break a chair over the pulpit in illustrating a point. Other times he would glide across the stage as if he were sliding into home plate to illustrate going to heaven. One biographer called Billy Sunday, "God's joke on the ministry."

One time Billy Sunday was preaching and carrying on in his unusual and yet usual way. He began to preach "hell hot, heaven sweet, sin black, judgment sure, and Jesus saves," and the power of God fell. He gave the invitation and hundreds of people "hit the sawdust trail" to trust Jesus Christ as their Lord.

One of the people who came forward that evening was an old man with a long white beard. He was standing near the platform to give his heart to Jesus. For some reason, Billy Sunday was fascinated with that man's beard; he couldn't get his eyes off of it.

Finally, temptation got the better of him and Billy Sunday went over to the edge of that platform, bent over, grabbed that man's beard, pulled it and said, "Honk, honk!" Now, in my wildest imagination I could never dream of doing something like that, and I don't know a preacher that would. Yet, Billy Sunday did it, and God used him to win over a million souls to Jesus Christ.

God calls people that the world would never call. God called a timid man with a stutter—a speech impediment—by the name of Moses and made him the greatest leader in the Old Testament. God called David, a little shepherd boy, right out of the pasture and made him the greatest king who ever ruled over Israel. God called Amos, a country farmer without any education, and made him one of the greatest prophets in all of the Bible. God's ways are above our ways, His thoughts are above our thoughts, and His calling confounds the wise. God calls the foolish.

God Calls the Feeble

God has chosen "the weak things of the world to put to shame the things which are mighty." The word here for weak means "physically weak, handicapped without strength." You may not have great physical strength or athletic ability. You may not have mountains of muscles or bulging biceps. But the only thing that matters to God is that every inch and ounce of you be given over completely to Jesus Christ.

Someone has said, "It doesn't take much of a man to be a Christian. It just takes all that there is of him." God takes the weak, feeble, sick, infirm, handicapped, and shames those things which are strong.

When I think of the weak I recall the life of Jonathan Edwards. He was one of the greatest revival preachers America or the world has ever known. Edwards once preached a message called "Sinners in the Hand of an Angry God," perhaps the most famous sermon in American history.

He was an asthmatic. Whenever he would preach he would cough and hack and wheeze during most of the message. He was a very thin, frail man. He had horrible eyesight. Jonathan Edwards read his messages. He read them in a monotone and read them at a very low volume because his voice was very weak.

His eyesight was so poor that not only did he wear thick glasses, but to read his sermons he would have to hold the messages about an inch from his nose. His sermons would last over two hours because of these conditions. But Jonathan Edwards' sermons, despite his disabilities, caused people to come writhing in anguish down the aisles wanting to get right with God. That frail, thin, little stick became the match that God used to light the fire of revival all over America.

Then I think about Fanny Crosby. Many of our favorite hymns were written by her. What you may not know is that Fanny Crosby was accidentally blinded when she was six years of age by an ignorant doctor who put hot poultice wraps on her inflamed eyes. Yet even in her blindness God used Fanny Crosby to write over 1,000 hymns.

God Calls the Familiar

God calls the "base things of the world and the things which are despised." The word "base" means exactly the opposite of the word "noble" in verse 26. It means "to be of low birth, ignoble without pedigree"—just an ordinary, run-of-the-mill, normal, everyday person. Were you not born with a silver spoon in your mouth? Are you not from the aristocracy? Wonderful. You are most likely to be used in the kingdom of God.

You may be like that fellow who said, "I wasn't born in a log cabin like some of the great men of our country. But just as soon as our family could afford one we bought it and moved in." Maybe you were born on the other side of the tracks. Perhaps you had to ride in the back of the bus. Was your clothing always a little less fancy than the other kids? If so, you are exactly the kind of person God is looking for.

When God was looking for the first King of Israel, He chose

Saul. When the priest Samuel came to Saul to give him instructions and to reveal God's will, Saul said, "Am I not a Benjamite, of the smallest of the tribes of Israel, and my family the least of all the families of the tribe of Benjamin? Why then do you speak like this to me?" (1 Sam. 9:21)

Saul was saying, "This is not logical. Of all the tribes in Israel, Benjamin is the smallest. Of all the families in Benjamin, my family is the least. Why in the world would you want me?" Samuel had to say to him, "Saul, that is just the point. You are just low enough that God can use you."

I think about the story of Gideon. Now you talk about a nobody. Gideon lived in a time of great trouble in Israel. The enemy Midianites had overrun the land with all of their army. Gideon was threshing wheat when the angel of the Lord appeared to him and said, "The Lord is with you, you mighty man of valor. Go in this might of yours, and you shall save Israel from the hands of the Midianites" (Jud. 6:12, 14).

Now when the angel of the Lord said this, Gideon looked around to make sure he was talking with him. When it dawned on Gideon that he was being called a mighty man of valor, he said, "O my Lord, how can I save Israel? Indeed my clan is the weakest in Manasseh, and I am the least in my father's house" (Jud. 6:15).

Now Gideon, like Saul, was saying something like: "You have the wrong man. Of all the tribes in Israel, Manasseh is the worst, and of all the families in Manasseh my family is the poorest. Of all the kids in my family, I am the runt of the litter." But the angel of the Lord said, "That's just the point. You are just low enough that I can use you." If you remember the story, God made Gideon reduce the size of his army to 300 soldiers. He then took a nobody general and a nothing army and defeated the Midianites. God gave Israel the victory, and He got the glory.

It is the ordinary, everyday run-of-the-mill nobodies that God uses the most. Abraham Lincoln said, "God must love the common people, because He made so many of them." There is a tremendous lesson to learn in these verses. Everybody, especially the nobody, is somebody in His body.

GOD'S CALLING IS PURPOSEFUL

Now why is it that God primarily uses the nobodies rather than the somebodies? Why does God use the foolish and not the wise? Why the feeble instead of the strong? Why the base things rather than the noble? Well, when God's calling is so particular and so peculiar, it winds up being so purposeful.

It Eliminates Our Pride

"That no flesh should glory in His presence" says 1 Corinthians 1:29, completing the idea of verse 28. There is no bragging in heaven, just praise. You can't brag on how you got to heaven; it is all by God's grace. You can't brag on what you did for God before you got to heaven, because it was all of God's calling. God is in the business of getting glory for Himself and the Bible says God will not share His glory with another. God will only use you if you are willing to give Him all the glory for the way He does use you, and if you ever quit giving Him the glory, He will quit using you.

Don't become like the woodpecker who was pecking away on a Georgia pine and was stunned by a bolt of lightning that split the tree from top to bottom. He could hardly believe his eyes. He backed off, looked at that tree for a moment and flew away. He came back later, leading nine other woodpeckers, and with a great deal of swagger and pride, pointed to the tree and said, "There it is, gentlemen, right over there." Remember, no pride, just praise in the kingdom of God.

It Elevates Our Position

"But of Him you are in Christ Jesus" (1 Cor. 1:30). It is not who you are, nor what you are that is important. It is whose you are and where you are that counts. The key to spiritual greatness is not your vocation—what you do. It is your location—where you are.

Greatness is not a matter of power, pride, prestige, or possessions. Greatness is a matter of position. You are either in Christ, or you are out of luck as far as being used by the Lord. God is not impressed with what you can do for Him. God is only concerned with what He can do through you.

It Exposes Our Power

"Who became for us wisdom from God—and righteousness and sanctification and redemption" (1 Cor. 1:30). Jesus is our wisdom, righteousness, sanctification, and redemption. To be used of God all you need is to be full of Jesus. We have been saved from the penalty of sin, that is our righteousness. We are being saved from the power of sin, that is our sanctification. And we will be saved from the presence of sin, that is our redemption.

Jesus gave Himself for us in order that He might give Himself to us and therefore, live His life through us. The Christian life is not so much our responsibility as it is our response to His ability. Jesus doesn't need you to serve Him. You need Jesus in order to serve Him.

A missionary came home after many years of foreign service and a young man asked her, "In all those years of service, what's the greatest lesson you learned?" The missionary responded, "I learned that Jesus is not only necessary, Jesus is enough." All you need to serve Jesus is Jesus.

It Evokes Our Praise

This passage closes with, "That, as it is written, 'He who glories, let him glory in the Lord' " (1 Cor. 1:31). What a wonderful plan this is. God takes an ordinary person, fills him with "superordinary" power, uses him in an extraordinary way, and we get the blessing and God gets the glory.

The people that God uses and chooses, God's all-stars, are not people of *ability*; they are people of *availability* who have learned the secret of giving their praise to God. If you use your life for the glory of God, God will use your life for His glory.

Perhaps the greatest composer of all time was Johann Sebastian Bach. According to history, he often put the letters S-D-G on his compositions. No one knew what they meant until late in his life it was discovered that they stood for the Latin words *soli deo gloria*. In English that means "to God alone be the glory."

God's all-stars are simply the nobodies of this life who are willing to spend their lives for the glory of God. If you do this, the Lord promises spiritual health and wholeness.

THE

Part **+** *Two*

WALK

OF A

HEALTHY

CHRISTIAN

●

ONE THING EVERY CHRISTIAN OUGHT TO KNOW

The ancient philosopher Socrates said, "Knowledge is the one good; and ignorance is the one evil." Though I believe he may have overstated his case, his point is still well taken. Nothing can be as damaging or as dangerous as ignorance. Contrary to popular opinion, what you don't know *can* hurt you.

An ambassador from Spain, who did not know the English language very well, came to America to serve his country. He met up with an American diplomat, and they began to engage in conversation. The American asked the ambassador if he had any children. The ambassador tried to explain that unfortunately his wife could not have a child.

The ambassador said, "My wife is *impregnable*." Looking at the face of the American, he knew that was not quite the right word, and so he offered, "What I mean is my wife is *inconceivable*." That obviously made matters worse, and he thought for a moment and finally triumphantly said, "What I'm trying to say is, my wife is *unbearable*." The man was trapped by his own ignorance. There are many Christians just like this man who are trapped by their own spiritual ignorance.

Jesus said, "You shall know the truth, and the truth will make you free" (John 8:32). Notice it is not just the truth that sets you free; it is knowing the truth that sets you free.

There is one truth that every Christian ought to know, and it is this: *your body is the temple of the Holy Spirit* (1 Cor. 6:19). It is interesting to notice that the word *your* is plural, while the word *body* is singular. It is as if Paul is talking to an entire congregation at once but pointing out each person individually and saying, "Your body, sir, your body, lady, your body, Christian teenager, your body, little child, if you are saved, is a temple of the Holy Spirit." I believe that if the average Christian could get hold of the importance and the implications of this one truth, it could radically transform his or her life.

The Spiritual Presence in the Body

Every Christian's body is a temple of the Holy Spirit. There is a false teaching going around in certain circles today that being saved and receiving the Holy Spirit are two different experiences. First you get saved. Then later on in some kind of mystical experience you receive the Holy Spirit.

The problem with that teaching is if you don't have the Holy Spirit you cannot possibly be a Christian in the first place. The Bible teaches, "If anyone does not have the Spirit of Christ, he is not His" (Rom. 8:9). When you are saved you receive the Holy Spirit or else you are not saved.

But we need to understand that the Holy Spirit is not only a power that comes upon us; it is a Person who comes to live within us. There is so much talk about the power of the Holy Spirit, and we all should have the fullness of the Spirit's power. But I want you to know that just as important as having the fullness of the Spirit's power, is having the fullness of the Spirit's presence.

Our body is a temple of the Holy Spirit. Keep in mind that the temple in the Bible was a place of worship. We need to understand our body, as a temple of the Holy Spirit, is also to be a place of worship. The Holy Spirit lives in my temple twenty-four hours a day. Therefore, every waking moment of every day my body is to be a place of worship. You don't come to church to worship, you bring your worship with you. Your body is a temple of the Holy Spirit twenty-four hours a day, seven days a week, fifty-two weeks a year.

Your body is not a hotel with checkout time at 12:00 noon Sunday. Your body is a temple where the Spirit of God resides every moment of every day. This principle tells me how I ought to treat my body.

It Is to Be a Holy Body

When I speak of the body as being holy, that does not mean we ought to worship it. People go to two extremes when it comes to how they treat their bodies. Some people *ignore* their bodies. They let their bodies run down like an abandoned shack. They let them get fat, flabby, and floppy, treating their stomachs like garbage disposals. They look like a "before" picture in a health club advertisement.

But on the other hand there are some who go to the other extreme and *idolize* their bodies. They run, pump iron, take vitamins, and eat wheat germ to make their bodies healthier and stronger. There is nothing wrong with taking care of the body, but you can go to an extreme.

I do not believe we ought to ignore the body, but I don't believe we ought to idolize it either. I believe the truth lies in the middle. There ought to be a real respect for our bodies. We think of a church building as a sanctuary that's holy, set apart for the Lord. Men come in and take their hats off out of respect. We may teach our children not to be boisterous or frivolous in the church building because we call it the house of God.

In reality, a building is not the house of God. You are the house of God. You ought to have more respect for your body than you do for any building. Think about the maintenance and care that goes into keeping up church buildings. We ought to give maintenance, care, respect, and love to our bodies as temples of the Holy Spirit. They ought to be treated as holy bodies, set apart for the glory of God.

It Is to Be a Healthy Body

A body that has been set apart for God's glory ought to be a healthy body. The fact that your body is a temple of the Holy

Spirit should take care of the problem of tobacco once and for all. This year 340,000 Americans will die because of tobacco-related illnesses. It ought to go without saying that a Christian should not smoke. God's Holy Spirit does not want His temple filled with smoke.

A man asked me, "Do you believe that a Christian will go to heaven if he smokes?" I replied, "I not only believe that, I believe he will get there much quicker!" I am simply saying that if your body is a temple of the Holy Spirit it should not be defiled with tobacco.

First Corinthians 6:19 not only takes care of smoking, it also warns against gluttony. It is just as wrong to stuff God's temple with food as it is to stuff God's temple with smoke. Someone has said that "we dig our graves with our fork, embalm ourselves with alcohol, and lay a tobacco wreath on the grave." Rather than eating to live, too many of us live to eat.

That is why the Apostle Paul said, "Foods for the stomach and the stomach for foods, but God will destroy both it and them" (1 Cor. 6:13). That is, don't make a god out of your belly. Our bodies are to be *temples* of the Holy Spirit, not warehouses.

We ought to strive to have healthy bodies not so that we will live longer, but so that we will live better. A sound mind and a sound heart live much better in a sound body.

THE SACRIFICIAL PURCHASE OF THE BODY

"For you were bought at a price" (1 Cor. 6:20). The reason why God the Spirit lives in our bodies is because God the Son has bought our bodies. This speaks of our redemption. The word bought comes from the Greek word meaning "marketplace," and it refers to how a slave on the block in the marketplace would be bought, paid for, and given his freedom. We were once in the sin market, slaves to iniquity, but Jesus paid for us and set us free. This redemptive purchase brings three things into focus.

A Terrific Price Was Paid
First of all, we were bought at a price. What was that price?

Peter writes, "You were not redeemed with corruptible things like silver or gold . . . but with the precious blood of Christ" (1 Peter 1:18-19). The price was nothing less than the rich, red, royal blood of the King of kings and Lord of lords.

Remember, the grace of God is free, but it isn't cheap. True freedom is never free. We are free today because valiant, courageous men of years gone by shed their blood that we might have freedom. Likewise, Jesus paid with His own blood for the freedom that we now enjoy from sin, Satan, judgment, and hell. Jesus paid for our debt, putting us forever in His debt.

Jesus paid a terrific price for you and me: His own blood. An old Puritan once said, "Jesus paid for us with His own blood. The question is, 'Is He getting His money's worth?' " Think about the terrific price that was paid for your spiritual freedom.

A Terrible Pain Was Endured

Secondly, not only was our redemption at a high price, but the blood of Jesus came at a high price. I don't believe the most brilliant mind in the world can understand the agony, pain, and suffering that our Lord endured before and during the Cross. It began in Gethsemane. While a world slept, Jesus prayed. The Lamb that was slain before the world was now to be crucified for the world. In that garden was an agony almost greater than even the Son of God could bear.

Luke tells us that Jesus literally sweated drops of blood (Luke 22:44). Doctors describe this very rare phenomenon as "hemathidrosis" or "bloody sweat." Under great emotional stress tiny capillaries in the sweat glands can break, mixing sweat with blood. This process is so traumatic it can cause a person to go into shock and even cardiac arrest. The agony that Jesus bore on this night was so great that Luke tells us an angel had to come from heaven and minister to Him and strengthen Him.

He was then taken by force before a vicious and violent crowd. He was beaten with bamboo rods. He was struck in the face until no doubt every tooth was loosened. His beard was plucked as He experienced indescribable pain.

Then, a most terrible thing took place known as the scourging. Jesus was stripped of His clothing. Totally naked, His hands were tied to a post above His head. The Roman legionnaire stepped forward with a flagellum in his hand. It is a short whip consisting of several heavy thongs with two small balls of lead and bone attached near the end. Again and again Jesus' back was struck.

At first the heavy thongs cut through the skin only, but then as the blows continued, they cut deeper into muscle, and then into veins, until finally the skin of the back was hanging in long ribbons and the entire body was an unrecognizable mass of torn, bleeding tissue.

Then a wreath of thorns, some thorns being up to an inch long, as sharp as razors, was jammed down onto His scalp. His tormentors literally hammered this crown of thorns into the flesh and almost into the skull itself.

At this time Jesus was literally unrecognizable. We see pictures of Jesus on the cross, and there is just a trickle of blood coming from His head. But this is a misrepresentation. Had you seen Jesus before He was hanged on the Cross, you would not have recognized Him. Isaiah 52:14 says, "His visage was marred more than any man."

The persecutors then took this broken body and hanged it on a rough-hewn timber. They took nails as big as railroad spikes and drove these nails deep into both wrists and into both feet. There every nerve of His body felt searing pain flashing through it hour after hour. Jesus was struggling every minute just to catch His breath. He raised up on His feet so He could exhale, but the pain was too great and when He had to slump forward He could not inhale. The picture is gruesome, but I am trying to show the tremendous pain endured for your freedom.

Yet that was not the greatest pain of all. The greatest suffering was not physical, it was spiritual. The greatest pain was the pain of separation, when even God turned His back on His own Son. Do you realize what happened in that very moment when God forsook His Son? For the only time in history, God did not walk through the valley of the shadow of death with one of His own children. The only child of God who ever had to walk through that death valley alone was Jesus Christ.

I agree with Martin Luther who said, "Our suffering is not worthy of the name of suffering. When I consider my crosses, tribulations, and temptations, I shame myself almost to death thinking what are they in comparison of the sufferings of my blessed Saviour, Jesus Christ."

A Total Possession Was Obtained

Thirdly, because of this purchase, "you are not your own" (1 Cor. 6:19). God owns you. He not only owns you lock, stock, and barrel, He owns you liver, spleen, and brain. Every part of you belongs to the Lord.

You can no longer say, "They are my lungs, I'll smoke if I want to." They are not your lungs. "They are my eyes, I will see what I want to." They are not your eyes. "It is my mouth, I will say what I please." It is not your mouth. You have been bought with a price. You are no longer your own.

God has two claims on every one of His children: He has the claim of creation, and He has the claim of redemption. God owns you because He made you and because He bought you.

I read of a boy who made a little red sailboat. He put that boat in a pond and due to carelessness it sailed away from him and he lost it.

Later on he was walking by a secondhand store and saw that same little red sailboat. He went in to ask for the boat but the proprietor would not give it to him. He made the boy buy it.

The boy went home, got all of his savings, came back, and bought back the little red boat. He hugged that little boat to his bosom as he walked home and he said, "Little sailboat, you are mine. You are twice mine. You are mine because I made you, and you are mine because I bought you." That is the same claim God has upon you.

THE SPECIAL PURPOSE FOR THE BODY

Finally, Paul says, "Therefore, glorify God in your body" (1 Cor. 6:20). Because God the Spirit lives within us and God the Son has paid for us, we ought to live to glorify God the Father. We have been put here for one purpose and that is to glorify God. "The chief end of man is to glorify God and enjoy Him forever." We were not created primarily to serve God, we were created primarily to glorify God. God says, "Everyone who is called by My name, I have created for My glory" (Isa. 43:7).

God did not create you for your good. He created you for His glory. God did not save you primarily to bless you. He saved you primarily to be blessed by you.

First Corinthians 10:31 says, "Therefore, whatever you eat or drink, or whatever you do, do all to the glory of God." Everything you say with your lips, see with your eyes, hear with your ears, taste with your mouth, and do with your hands, is to bring glory to God.

We get our word "doxology" from the word glorify. A doxology is a word of praise. That is what your body is to be to the Lord every day. It is to be a walking, living, breathing, talking testimony of praise and glory to our Heavenly Father. We ought to say with Francis R. Havergal each day:

> Take my life, and let it be
> Consecrated, Lord, to Thee;
> Take my hands, and let them move
> At the impulse of Thy love.
>
> Take my feet, and let them be
> Swift and beautiful for Thee;
> Take my voice, and let me sing
> Always, only, for my King.
>
> Take my love, my God I pour
> At Thy feet its treasure store;
> Take myself, and I will be
> Ever, only, all for Thee.

There is one test, an infallible, incontrovertible, inerrant test as to whether or not a given thing is right or wrong: Will it bring glory to God? This is the first and last question we must ask.

Remember, your body is a temple of the Holy Spirit. You have been bought with a price, therefore, whatever you do or say should bring glory to God. For whenever God gets the glory He deserves, we will have the blessing and the victory that we desire as His children.

CHAPTER

HOW TO BE HAPPY WHETHER MARRIED OR SINGLE

F O U R

Chances are you've never met me but I already know something about you: You are either married or single. We have all been hatched but we have not all been hitched, and you are either singing a duet or a solo.

Now I suspect something about some of you. I suspect that some of you are married but wish you were single. That reminds me of the boy who took a history exam where the final question was, "Who was Patrick Henry?" The little boy wrote, "Patrick Henry was a man who got married and then said, 'Give me liberty or give me death.' "

Further, I suspect very strongly that some of you are single but wish you were married. You are on the lookout for "Mr. Wonderful" or "Miss America" to settle down with and live happily ever after. But whether you are married or single, you can be happy in the Lord Jesus Christ. Through the inspiration of the Holy Spirit, the Apostle Paul has some advice and some admonition both to the married and the single person.

WISE WORDS FOR THE WEDDED LIFE

Much of 1 Corinthians 7 is spent dealing with the relationship of husband and wife. Here the Apostle Paul is giving advice on how to have a happy, holy, healthy, and harmonious marriage.

The first few verses read like a "Dear Abby" column as Paul responds to questions about married and single life that the Corinthians had evidently written to him. We see in the opening, "Now concerning the things of which you wrote to me" (1 Cor. 7:1). But there are two major differences between what we read here and what you might read in an advice column. First of all, this is not a newspaper column, this is the Word of God.

Secondly, we are not reading the words of one dependent upon human reasoning. These are the words of an inspired author who has received divine revelation. This is not just good advice; it is godly admonition. It deals with the intimate relationship between husband and wife. It goes to the very heart of the matter—the love and affection that bonds a man and woman. Paul is dealing primarily with the sexual relationship. He gives four pieces of advice on how to enter a happy marriage and keep it that way.

Reserve Affection for One Another

"It is good for a man not to touch a woman. Nevertheless, because of sexual immorality, let each man have his own wife, and let each woman have her own husband" (1 Cor. 7:1-2). God here tells us everything we need to know about sex. The passage is concerned with the fulfillment of the sexual drive. There is a divine plan for fulfilling the natural drives and desires that he has placed within men and women. That divine plan can be summed up in one word—marriage.

Sex was never intended for a man and a woman. Sex was intended only for a husband and a wife. Hebrews 13:4 states, "Marriage is honorable among all, and the bed undefiled; but fornicators and adulterers God will judge." Sex was God's idea. It is a creation of God. But when God created the sex act, He put boundaries around it. Sex is like a train. It is wonderful when it stays within the tracks, but it is terrible when it jumps them. The train of sex was meant to run between the track of a husband and a wife.

Only one person has a right to your body and that is the husband or wife God has intended for you to marry. God wants sex to be wonderful, not wicked. Sex within marriage is delightful, but sex without marriage is destructive. Paul warns us, "Flee sexual immorality. Every sin that a man does is outside the body, but he who commits sexual immorality sins against his own body" (1 Cor. 6:18).

Here is a profound yet simple solution to the sexual revolution. Every man is to have his own wife, and every woman is to have her own husband. We have complicated the simple, while God has simplified the complicated. We are spending hundreds of millions of dollars trying to find cures for AIDS. We are spending hundreds of millions of dollars trying to educate our young people and advertise contraceptives on television, when God tells us a very simple formula that is absolutely free and absolutely foolproof.

Here is God's solution: *virginity before marriage, monogamy after marriage.* That is it. No sex before marriage, all sex within marriage, no sex without marriage.

Now that does not mean that God is trying to keep you from sex. On the contrary, God is trying to keep sex for you. People enjoy sex more and enjoy more sex when it is within the confines of a monogamous marriage. If you are single, reserve your affection for that husband or wife God has chosen for you.

Receive Affection from One Another

"Let the husband render to his wife the affection due her, and likewise also the wife to her husband" (1 Cor. 7:3). Here we move from premarital to postmarital concerns. Once married, husbands and wives need to remember that love and affection are things that they owe one another. The husband is to render to his wife the affection due her.

You owe your mate both physical and verbal affection. The verb "render" is in the present tense, meaning you always owe this. This is a debt that you never pay off. The problem in many marriages today is the husband and wife have gotten deeply in debt, and they are behind in payments. We have husbands and wives today who are in arrears in the love and affection they owe to each other.

Many husbands complain that they do not have a romantic wife. The best way to have a romantic wife is to be a romantic husband. Unfortunately, we have picked up the idea that when a marriage begins the courtship ends. *Courtship should never end.* Husband, what you did to get her you ought to do to keep her.

Every woman likes to be courted. Just because you are married doesn't mean that you have to quit dating. As a matter of fact, real dating doesn't even begin until after you get married. Men, you need to court that wife and constantly remind her that she is the only woman in your life. Someone has observed that "the bonds of matrimony will surely go into default when the interest is not kept up."

But the wife must not be left out, because the wife is also to render affection unto her husband. The best way to have a romantic husband is to be a romantic wife. Courtship is a two-way street. Romance doesn't begin in the bedroom, but at the breakfast table. An atmosphere of love is created by looking and being the best you can be amidst life's daily routines.

Release Affection to One Another

"The wife does not have authority over her own body, but the husband does. And likewise the husband does not have authority over his own body, but the wife does. Do not deprive one another except with consent for a time, that you may give yourselves to fasting and prayer; and come together again so that Satan does not tempt you because of your lack of self-control" (1 Cor. 7:4-5). These verses offer suggestions on practicing marital fidelity. It is a very simple principle, probably one that is violated more than any other principle in marriage. There is to be an exchange of authority. The wife does not have authority over her body, nor does the husband have authority over his, but they have authority over each other. If wives and husbands would remember that one principle there would be greater sexual and marital harmony in the home.

When you marry you gain something, but you also lose something. You gain a mate, but you lose a body. Wife, your body no longer belongs to you, it belongs to him. Husband, your body no longer belongs to you, it belongs to her. Sex is not something that is to be forcibly taken, it is something that is to be lovingly given.

Sex is not just for procreation, nor is it primarily even for recreation. Sex is a gift of God given for communication. In the Old Testament, whenever a man would have relations with his wife it was described, for example as, "Adam knew Eve his wife" (Gen. 4:1). The word "knew" referred to the marriage act. You see, the marriage act is the most intimate form of communication known to humans.

Retain Affection with One Another

"Now to the married I command, yet not I but the Lord: A wife is not to depart from her husband. But even if she does depart, let her remain unmarried or be reconciled to her husband. And a husband is not to divorce his wife" (1 Cor. 7:10-11). If you have ever wondered what the Bible teaches about divorce and remarriage, a basic summary is found in these verses. The basic biblical teaching is a wife is not to depart from the husband, and a husband is not to divorce his wife. But if they do divorce one another, they are both to remain unmarried.

As if to underscore the strength of this teaching, Paul goes on to outline a situation where two people are married but one mate later is saved. Evidently, there was a question as to whether or not that was a basis to divorce the unsaved mate.

But the teaching even then is that divorce is out of the question if the unsaved mate is willing to live with a person who is saved. We are told in 1 Corinthians 7:14 that "the unbelieving husband is sanctified by the wife, and the unbelieving wife is sanctified by the husband; otherwise your children would be unclean, but now they are holy."

The word sanctified here refers to the blessing of God. One Christian in a marriage will cause the blessing of God to be on that home. It will cause the children of that home to be blessed by the Lord.

But the emphasis of this entire passage is that marriage is not to be until *debt* do you part, or until *doubt* do you part, but until *death* do you part. That is why the chapter concludes in verse 39 by saying "a wife is bound by law as long as her husband lives."

STRONG STANDARDS FOR THE SINGLE LIFE

Although the church, to its shame and discredit, has often forgotten the single person, God has not. Between 1970 and 1982 the single population of this country rose 78 percent from 11 million to 19 million. One-third of this group or almost 6 million people have never been married. One group that the church needs to address today is that group of "swinging singles." Regardless of the church's response, God has set some strong standards for the single life.

A Proper Life
The single life is a *good* life. Paul says in verse 1, "It is good for a man not to touch a woman." The word touch there refers to the marriage act. We are not told that the single life is the best life or the better life, but it is a good life. It is a proper life.

There is nothing wrong with being single. If we see a beautiful woman or a handsome man who is not married we may think, "I wonder what is wrong with her, or what is wrong with him?" In fact, nothing at all may be wrong with that person. Indeed, something might be wrong with them if they were married. It is better to be a single than to marry the wrong person.

There are some things that are worse, indeed much worse, than being single. Two friends were sitting next to one another on a bus when the one man noticed that his friend was wearing a wedding ring on the index finger of his right hand. Now most people wear their wedding rings on the ring finger of their left hand.

The man said, "That's strange. Is that your wedding ring?"

He replied, "Yes."

The man questioned, "Why are you wearing it on the wrong finger of the wrong hand?"

"Well," the pundit responded, "I married the wrong woman."

The single life is not only a good life, it is a *gifted* life. Paul says, "I wish that all men were even as I myself. But each one has his own gift from God, one in this manner and another in that" (1 Cor. 7:7). Singleness is a gift, and some people have the gift and some people do not.

Jesus said that some people would have the gift of being single, "For there are eunuchs who are born thus from their mother's womb, and there are eunuchs who were made eunuchs by men, and there are eunuchs who have made themselves eunuchs for the kingdom of heaven's sake. He who is able to accept it, let him accept it" (Matt. 19:12).

That does not mean that being single makes you more spiritual than if you were married. The last thing any church needs is a comparison between the spiritual singles and the carnal couples.

The fact of the matter is, that some people have been chosen and gifted by the Lord to be single. I believe God calls most people to be married, but not all people. There are some people who have been given the gift of being single, and it is a gift. That is what makes it a proper life. No person should ever be ashamed or embarrassed because he or she is single.

A Productive Life

Why is it that certain people are gifted to be single? So that they can serve the Lord without any hindrances. A married man may serve the Lord just as effectively as a single man. But a single man may be able to serve the Lord easier than a married man.

First of all, a single may serve the Lord without *distress*. Paul says that the single life "is good because of the present distress" (1 Cor. 7:26). That is, in many ways it is easier as a single person to handle the troubles of this world.

For example, if a single person loses his job he doesn't have to worry about a wife and children to feed like a married man does. He doesn't have the expenses of a married man. You have heard people say that two can live as cheaply as one. That is true if one of them doesn't eat! The only financial bargain you will find in a marriage is the marriage license. The price goes up after that.

A single may also serve without *distraction.* Later Paul says in verse 35 of the chapter, "This I say for your own profit, not that I may put a leash on you, but for what is proper, and that you may serve the Lord without distraction."

A married man must be double-minded. He has to worry not only about pleasing the Lord, but about pleasing his wife. As a matter of fact, a married man cannot be faithful to the Lord, if he is not faithful to his family.

A single person has no such worries. In fact, if you are single this ought to be one of the most productive times in your life. You have time that the married person does not have to serve the Lord. You will have undivided energy. Indeed, some of the most productive people who have ever lived were singles. The greatest Man who ever walked the face of this earth was sin-gle—His name was Jesus. The greatest missionary who ever lived was a single—his name was Paul.

A Pure Life

A man or woman ought to remain single if possible, but if they cannot control their sexual desire they ought to marry. "It is better to marry than to burn with passion" (1 Cor. 7:9).

The great danger to the single life is the sex life. You may be a single without the gift of being single. You may right now be filled with desire. There is nothing wrong with that. That fire in you, the desire, is a God-given drive. It is nothing to be ashamed or afraid of.

There are singles this moment who are on the verge of an urge to merge. There is a fire burning down in you. Well, there is nothing wrong with a fire as long as it burns under control.

If you don't have this gift of being single it is all right to seek a mate. Proverbs 18:22 says, "He who finds a wife finds a good thing, and obtains favor from the Lord." If you are in the mate-hunting business that is all right with God.

One pastor was preaching on marriage from the first chapter of Genesis. He was very firm and adamant that "God's plan is one woman for one man till death do them part."

After the service he was met by a young woman who was very perturbed. She said, "Pastor, I want to talk to you about this business of one woman for one man till death do them part."

He asked, "Don't you agree with it?"

She responded, "Oh yes, I agree with it. I just want to get in on it!"

If you want to get in on marriage, that is perfectly all right with God.

Let me give you a couple of hints on how to do it in a godly way. If I could give a single person one piece of advice it would be this: Before you can *find* the right person, you have to *be* the right person. Marriage is more than finding the right person; it is being the right person.

You ought to get so right with God, so in tune with Him, that your potential mate will be spiritually attracted to you. But not only must you be the right person, you need to look for the right person. Do not, under any circumstances, date or marry a non-Christian. Second Corinthians 6:14 makes it plain that a believer and an unbeliever are not to be unequally yoked.

Then you need to look in the right place. You are not likely to find the kind of man or woman you are looking for in a bar or some singles' club. I believe the best place to find God's mate for your life is in a church. If your mate was not in church before you met him, chances are he won't be in church after you marry him.

Finally, when you marry do it for the right purpose. The primary purpose for marriage is to bring glory to God. If you cannot look at that mate and say, "I know this marriage is going to be one that honors our Lord," then you should never ever marry.

This is God's prescription. Whether you are married or single, you can be happy if (1) Jesus Christ is your Lord, (2) your body is being preserved as a temple of the Holy Spirit, and (3) your spiritual state is placed above your marital status.

TURNING TEMPTATION INTO TRIUMPH

It affects everybody. It has no regard for custom, color, or creed. It cuddles up to the rich and to the poor. It stands with the intellectual; it sits with the illiterate. It is as much at home in a Cadillac with a rich man as it is on a bicycle with a poor man. It slights no race. It skips no generation.

It comes in all shapes, forms, and sizes. Sometimes it hides in a plate of food. It may be concealed in a bottle of liquor. Sometimes it walks on the two legs of a woman or a man.

It was the beginning of the downfall of the human race. It's the root of destruction in every marriage that fails and home that falls apart. Every Christian has to face it every day, and you can never get away from it. No matter how many times you knock it down, it stands right back up ready to fight another day.

What is it? It is *temptation*. Everybody faces temptation. Some people fight it. They try to resist it as best they can. Some people simply surrender to it. They let temptation have its way. The British writer, Oscar Wilde, summed up the attitude of most of us when he said, "I can resist anything except temptation."

You may be one of those people who feel helpless against temptation. There may be a certain temptation that is meeting you, beating you, and defeating you at every turn. You have fought it until you are tired. Now you are not only tired of the foe, you are tired of the fight. You feel so helpless. Well, there is hope for the hopeless. God has given to all of us a way that we can turn temptation into triumph.

RECOGNIZE THE REALITY OF TEMPTATION

What do we mean by temptation? Peter Lord gives the best definition I know: "Temptation is the devil trying to get you to fulfill a natural God-given desire or drive in the wrong way." That is a perfect definition.

It recognizes both the reality of a personal devil and the reality of the work that he does in trying to tempt us to do wrong. The best way to deal with a problem is to recognize the problem for what it is. The same thing is true in dealing with temptation. One needs to understand the reality of temptation. The Apostle Paul discusses some elements of temptation in 1 Corinthians 10.

A Common Reality

Paul tells us, "No temptation has overtaken you except such as is common to man" (1 Cor. 10:13). Temptation is almost as old as time itself. It began in the Garden of Eden when Eve was tempted by the serpent to disobey the Lord. From that very moment it has affected every person who has ever lived. The Bible says there is nothing new under the sun (Ecc. 1:9), and that includes temptation.

Everyone who has ever lived has been tempted, including the Lord Jesus Christ. Now temptation affects different people in different ways. Not everyone is tempted by the same thing or in the same way. What may tempt you may not tempt me.

For example, a beer does not tempt me because I do not drink. But it would easily tempt an alcoholic. My associate pastor loves popcorn and ice cream and has a real weakness for them. I could walk through a warehouse of freshly cooked popcorn or fall into a swimming pool full of ice cream, and it would not affect me because I don't care for them. But I have a tremendous weakness for Peanut M & M's. By the way, I handle that temptation by keeping a jar of them on my desk!

Now temptation, in and of itself, is not a sin. Shakespeare said, "It is one thing to be tempted and another thing to fall." Eve did not sin when she was tempted. She only sinned when she gave in to the temptation.

If temptation was a sin, then Jesus was a sinner for He "was in all points tempted as we are, yet without sin" (Heb. 4:15). Jesus was tempted just like you and I are tempted. The reason He was tempted was so that He could help us in our temptation. "For in that He Himself has suffered, being tempted, He is able to aid those who are tempted" (Heb. 2:18).

There is nothing wrong with temptation. There is nothing wrong with you if you are being tempted. As a matter of fact, there is something wrong with you if you are not tempted. A young single man sees a beautiful single girl and says, "I believe there is something wrong with me. Whenever I see a young woman like that I have certain feelings that wail up within me." That's perfectly normal. If he didn't have such desires he ought to go see a doctor! Those are God-given feelings, and there is nothing wrong with them. Temptation is a common reality.

A Continuous Reality

Temptation is something that is always with you. You will have to face this monster every day of your life. Many young Christians think that when they get saved they no longer have to face temptation. Do you believe the devil will leave you alone, and you will never be bothered with sin again? I have some news for you! When you get saved you will face more temptation than when you were lost.

If you have not been meeting the devil since you became a Christian, it is because you and he are walking in the same direction. Because when you are saved you begin to walk against the world. Your spirit begins to war against your flesh, and you become locked in combat with Satan, and he never lets up.

Dr. Vance Havner has said something that we need to learn

well: "Let it not be forgotten that a twice-born and Spirit-filled Christian is always a contradiction to this old world. He crosses it at every point. From the day that he is born again until he passes on to be with the Lord, he pulls against the current of a world forever going the other way. The real firebrand is distressing to the devil, and when a wide-awake believer comes along, taking the Gospel seriously, we can expect sinister maneuvering for his downfall" (*The Secret of Christian Joy,* Fleming H. Revell, 1938, p. 54).

Temptation never takes a vacation, and if you take a vacation it will go with you. Temptation will hit you when you are strongest and knock you down and kick you when you are weakest. That is why Paul said, "Let him who thinks he stands take heed lest he fall" (1 Cor. 10:12). George Heath's "My Soul Be on Thy Guard" says it well:

> My soul be on thy guard;
> Ten thousand foes arise;
> The hosts of sin are pressing hard
> To draw thee from the skies.
>
> Ne'er think the victory won,
> Nor lay thine armor down;
> The work of faith will not be done
> 'Til thou obtain the crown.

REJOICE IN THE RESTRAINT OF TEMPTATION

We go on to learn in verse 13, "But God is faithful, who will not allow you to be tempted beyond what you are able." I know two things. I know that I am going to be tempted, but I also know I am not going to face a temptation greater than I can bear, because God is faithful. "He shall deliver you in six troubles, yes, in seven no evil shall touch you" (Job 5:19).

God is faithful. He answers prayer. One prayer our Heavenly Father is sure to answer is this, "Do not lead us into temptation, but deliver us from the evil one" (Matt. 6:13).

God never leads us to temptation, but rather always delivers us from evil. God never tempts us to do wrong. You can never blame your sin on God. James 1:13 says, "Let no one say when he is tempted, 'I am tempted by God'; for God cannot be tempted by evil, nor does He Himself tempt anyone."

Don't try to justify your sin by exaggerating the strength of temptation or underestimating the power of God. I know that no temptation I face is stronger than my ability to bear it. God restrains temptation in that fashion.

That means you cannot say, "The devil made me do it." The devil cannot even make an unbeliever sin, much less a saint.

Think about it. If Satan could make you do anything wrong, he would make you do everything wrong. If he could make you sin some of the time, he would make you sin all of the time. If your sin was the devil's fault then God would have laid your sin on the devil. Instead of crucifying Jesus, He would have killed the devil. But that would have done no good.

If Satan died today you would still sin tomorrow. You can't blame your sin on the devil. You can't blame your sin on temptation. Nathaniel Willis wrote, "No degree of temptation justifies any degree of sin." You cannot blame your sin on God, the devil, temptation, or on others.

We are told not to leave the keys in our cars because we may tempt a young man to steal them. This sounds as if I happen to leave the keys in my auto and a young kid steals my car, then it is my fault. But does this make sense?

Suppose two young men walk down the street and see my keys in my car. The first young man sees my keys, but keeps right on walking. But the second young man sees my keys, gets in the car, and steals it. If I am to blame for the second kid stealing my car, why didn't the first kid do likewise?

People do not sin because they are tempted to sin. Temptation may be the beginning of sin, but it is not the cause of sin. Humans sin because they want to sin. People do not give into temptation because they have to, but because they want to. They do not give into temptation because they *can't* resist it, but because they *won't* resist it. Paul illustrated this principle with the Israelites in the Old Testament. He tells us in 1 Corinthians 10:11 that what happened to them occurred as examples for us, "They were written for our admonition." Look at the sins they committed. Verses 7-10 of chapter 10 describe the situation.

In verse 7 we are told they committed the sin of *idolatry.* "Do not become idolators as were some of them." They began to worship other gods, even as today we worship other gods. In that same verse we see that they also committed the sin of *indecency,* "The people sat down to eat and drink, and rose up to play." The word *play* there is a euphemism for sexual relationships. They got drunk on liquor and wine and began to engage in sexual orgies. Verse 8 describes their *immorality.* They began to swap husbands and wives and fall into all kinds of adulterous situations. In verses 9-10 we are told that they committed the sin of *infidelity.* They complained against the Lord, and they complained against their leadership.

Did they do all of this because they were tempted? No. They committed these sins because they wanted to. Paul says, "Now these things became our examples, to the intent that we should not lust after evil things as they also lusted" (v. 6).

Now notice the process. First they *lusted* in verse 6. Then in verses 7-10 they *sinned,* and then we are told in verse 10 they were *destroyed.* That is exactly the same process you find in the Book of James, "But each man is tempted, when he is drawn away of his own lust, and enticed. Then when lust hath conceived, it bringeth forth sin and sin when it is finished, bringeth forth death" (James 1:14-15, KJV). There you have it: lust, sin, and death—the LSD of the Bible.

Sin begins with temptation, but it is not caused by temptation. You can overcome whatever temptation you are facing because God restrains it. You will not be tempted beyond what you are able.

RELY ON THE REMEDY FOR TEMPTATION

God has not left us alone in our battle with temptation. What is God's plan? We are told that God "with the temptation will also make the way of escape, that you may be able to bear it" (1 Cor. 10:13). God's plan for turning temptation into triumph is not to *endure* temptation, but to *escape* temptation.

Remember we are dealing with temptation, not trials. It is temptation, not troubles. Again, we are facing temptation, not tribulation. We are to endure trials, troubles, and tribulation, but we are to escape temptation.

Many Christians get into deep difficulty because they try to do just the opposite, escaping trouble and enduring temptation. But if you try that you are going to wind up failing miserably at both.

First of all, you cannot escape trouble. "Man who is born of woman is of few days and full of trouble" (Job 14:1). "Man is born to trouble, as the sparks fly upward" (Job 5:7). Now you should not go out of your way looking for trouble. But don't try to avoid it if you are doing what God wants you to do.

You are not to escape trouble, but you are to escape temptation. Now if you try to escape trouble, you are a coward. But if you try to endure temptation, you are a fool. There are two simple prescriptions of divine advice on how to turn temptation into triumph.

First of all, *do not get into a tempting situation.* Too many people are like the little boy who was sitting under the farmer's apple tree. The farmer came out and asked, "Son, are you trying to steal an apple?" The little boy replied, "No sir, I'm trying not to." His problem was being under the tree in the first place. Someone has well said, "If you don't want to eat the devil's apples, stay out of his orchard."

Young people need to learn that the best way to avoid marrying a non-Christian is to not date one. You will be tempted to fall in love with anyone you date. Thus, the solution is to simply avoid tempting situations.

Martin Luther said, "You can't keep birds from flying over your head, but you can keep them from building nests in your hair." In other words, you may not keep pornography off the rack, but you can avoid going where it is sold, and you can avoid buying it.

I was on a plane once when the pilot came on the intercom and said, "Ladies and gentlemen, we have a terrible thunderstorm ahead of us, much thunder and lightning, heavy rain, high winds, and there could be a lot of turbulence involved. So I am going to veer west and fly around that storm even though it will cost us another twenty minutes." I remember thinking, "That's fine with me."

Now that pilot was not a coward for avoiding that storm. He would have been a fool for flying through it. I'm grateful that he avoided that storm. That is just what we need to do, avoid those storms of temptation that we see coming ahead.

The second piece of advice is this: *If you stumble into a tempting situation, get out of it quickly.* The Bible never says we are to fight temptation. The Bible says we are to flee temptation. Second Timothy 2:22 states, "Flee also youthful lusts." First Corinthians 6:18 warns, "Flee sexual immorality."

A perfect example of this principle is Joseph. You remember him, a young man who loved God, who was in Potiphar's house going about his servant duties when Potiphar's wife came in. This was not a situation that Joseph could have avoided. He just walked into it, or rather it walked into him. Potiphar's wife said something like, "Joseph, my old man's not around; it's just you and me here alone, and no one will ever know. Why don't you and I get together. I mean, after all, when the cat's away the mice will play." Joseph probably thought, "Well, the only problem is, I'm not a mouse." The Bible says he fled from there so quickly that he left his coat behind.

Some people would have laughed at him, but he did not give up his testimony, compromise his conscience, or do something that could have cost him his life. He stood true for God. You see, God had provided a way of escape. Many times the best way of escape is the King's highway, two legs, and a hard run.

As you walk the streets of life, from time to time you are going to turn corners. Many times when you do you're going to come face-to-face with temptation. Remember that when you do, God always has a way of escape. He is never early; He is never late. He does not provide an escape before the temptation, or after the temptation, but *with* the temptation He will make that way of escape (1 Cor. 10:13).

I was reading about a battle in which a king was allowing his eighteen-year-old son to lead the army for the first time. The prince's father had a strong force, and the king drew up nearby, watching the battle but taking no part.

The young prince began to be hard-pressed by the enemy, and he saw his forces get into considerable danger. Again and again he sent hurried appeals to his father for assistance, but with no reply.

Finally, the prince in desperation sent a messenger and said, "Will my father the king not help me in my time of need?" The king sent back this message: "Tell my son that I am not so inexperienced a commander as not to know when help is needed, and not so careless a father as not to send it when it is."

Our King and our Father watches us in our battle against temptation. He knows the danger far better than we do. When the time is right He will provide a way of escape. Second Peter 2:9 says, "The Lord knows how to deliver the godly out of temptations."

The world, the flesh, and the devil are against you, but God is for you. "If God is for us, who can be against us?" (Rom. 8:31) "Greater is He who is in you, than he that is in the world" (1 John 4:4, KJV). Horatio Palmer summed it up:

> Yield not to temptation
>   For yielding is sin;
> Each victory will help you
>   Some other to win;
> Fight manfully onward,
>   Dark passions subdue;
> Look ever to Jesus
>   He'll carry you through.

He will carry you through and turn your temptation into triumph.

Part  *Three*

THE

WORK

OF A

HEALTHY

CHRISTIAN

●

YOU ARE A GIFTED CHILD

Ignorance about spiritual gifts is perhaps the greatest infection that plagues Christians seeking to be healthy. God has graciously blessed His children with a wide array of gifts for their personal growth and corporate edification. Unfortunately, too many believers neglect our Heavenly Father's gifts. But if you are to be a growing, vibrant Christian—one who is the picture of spiritual health—you need to be aware of another one of God's prescriptions: spiritual gifts. In fact, I believe this topic to be of such importance to healthy Christians that I am devoting the six chapters in this section to an in-depth examination and exploration of spiritual gifts.

Spiritual gifts were obviously a hot topic at the church in Corinth, if we are to judge by the extent of Paul's discussion in 1 Corinthians. For our purposes here we'll again be focusing on the apostle's divine wisdom in that book, as well as some advice he offered in the Book of Romans.

It is interesting to note that one of the reasons Paul wrote to the Corinthians was because of their ignorance of spiritual gifts (1 Cor. 12:1). Now it is very easy to be ignorant of spiritual gifts, and I believe most Christians are. As a matter of fact, I am a Ph.D. graduate of a Southern Baptist Seminary. I went to a Southern Baptist college. I grew up in a Baptist Sunday School, and yet, I was never taught about spiritual gifts. Not one lecture or lesson was ever given on spiritual gifts.

But Paul warns us not to be ignorant of these gifts. From that Greek word for *ignorant* we get our word *agnostic*. Did you know that there are many spiritual agnostics, even in the church? There are some people who know about God, but they do not know God, and they are lost. But I'm afraid many Christians know God; that is, they are saved, but they do not know very much about God.

No Christian ever knows all about God that he ought to know. Every believer should continue to learn all that he or she can about who God is, and how He operates. God does not put a premium on ignorance.

There is a great cost involved in being educated, but there is a greater cost if you're not. That is especially true in regard to spiritual gifts. What you don't know can hurt you!

At this point, a caution needs to be made: Exercising spiritual gifts is no guarantee of having a great church. Nor is it a guarantee that you are spiritually mature.

The Corinthian church was well known for all the spiritual gifts that were manifested in their fellowship. As a matter of fact, Paul said to them, "You come short in no gift" (1 Cor. 1:7). All of the gifts were present and all of the gifts were being exercised. But Paul also said to them, "I, brethren, could not speak to you as to spiritual people but as to carnal, as to babes in Christ" (1 Cor. 3:2). They were exercising the gifts of the Spirit, but they were not exhibiting the fruit of the Spirit.

THE DESCRIPTION OF SPIRITUAL GIFTS

It is important to understand the nature and character of spiritual gifts. Paul's description is found in 1 Corinthians 12, which we'll be focusing on in this chapter. Notice in verse 1 that the word *gifts* is italicized in the *New King James Version*. That means it is not in the original language. The word there, *pneumatikon*, literally means "the spirituals." The translators inserted the word because they were trying to explain what they thought Paul meant. But actually the term simply means the "spirituals," that is, things pertaining to the Holy Spirit.

These gifts are from the Holy Spirit. Now all three persons in the Godhead have given us wonderful gifts. God the Father gave us Jesus the Son for our *salvation*. God the Son gave God the Holy Spirit for our *sanctification*. But God the Holy Spirit has given us spiritual gifts for our *service*.

They are not material gifts. The gifts of the Holy Spirit are not money, cars, clothes, or jewelry. Those are blessings from God, but they are not gifts of the Spirit; they are trinkets and toys. Spiritual gifts are treasures and tools. But remember, they are *spiritual* gifts.

They Are Supernatural Gifts

Paul tells us in verse 4, "There are diversities of gifts." Now the word for gifts here is different from the one used in verse 1. Here the word is *charismata*. The word *charis* literally means "grace." That is, these gifts are grace gifts. They are not only gifts of the Spirit, but they are gifts of grace.

Grace is a gift from God. You do not earn it, buy it, or work for it. You just accept it. The Bible says, "By grace you have been saved through faith" (Eph. 2:8). Just as you accept your salvation as a free gift from God, you are also to accept your spiritual gifts freely.

Spiritual gifts are supernatural. They are not just glorified natural abilities. They are not something you get by study, practice, or inheritance. They are charismatic gifts, grace gifts, given solely by God. If you are a Christian you are in the true sense of the term a charismatic Christian, because you have a gift of the Holy Spirit.

Spiritual gifts are supernatural endowments which enable us to carry out God's work in God's way. An atheist can give a stirring speech, but only a person with the gift of prophecy can preach a sermon. An infidel could give a lecture from a passage in the Bible, but only a person with the gift of teaching can rightly divide the Word of Truth. Barbra Streisand can sing "How Great Thou Art," but only a Sandi Patti, with the gift of exhortation, can sing it in such a way as to move people to God. Spiritual gifts are supernatural gifts.

They Are Service Gifts

Verse 7 tells us, "The manifestation of the Spirit is given to each one for the profit of all." Spiritual gifts are given to serve the church, to build up the body of Christ, and to edify the saints.

If a spiritual gift does not edify the church, it is no longer a *used* gift, it is an *abused* gift. Spiritual gifts are not given for your enjoyment, but for His employment. They are not toys for playing; they are tools for building. You will be blessed by exercising your spiritual gift, but it is not given primarily to bless you, but so that you might be a blessing to the body of Christ.

God not only wants you to serve Him; He wants you to serve Him the right way. There are many Christians who are trying to serve God, but are frustrated in trying to serve Him the wrong way. The best way to serve God—the right way because it is the only way—is to exercise your spiritual gift in the local church by the power of the Holy Spirit.

To try to serve God in any other way will lead to frustration and failure. Yet, you will never discover the true way until you realize that you were not meant to serve God in your flesh, but by the power of the Holy Spirit.

A young preacher, who is now a well-known author, years ago was in a very desperate condition. He was frustrated, feeling a failure in his ministry. He went to see the great preacher Ian Thomas. Major Thomas asked the young man, "What do you think God expects of you?"

As this young pastor thought of the high level of achievement that alone could please God, when he began to realize that God expects our very best, he became even more disconsolate and discouraged.

Then Major Thomas put his arm around the pastor and said, "Son, God expects nothing from you but failure!" Then he added, "But God has given the Holy Spirit to you so that you need not fail."

You too are to serve God, and you can serve God in such a way that is well pleasing in His sight by exercising your spiritual gifts in His service.

THE DISTRIBUTION OF SPIRITUAL GIFTS

Notice not only how spiritual gifts are described, but how they are distributed. "But one and the same Spirit works all these things, distributing to each one individually as He wills" (v. 11). Spiritual gifts are not given out arbitrarily, but under the sovereign control of the Holy Spirit.

They Are Distributed Individually

We are told in verse 11 that He distributes His gifts to "each one individually." Every Christian has received at least one spiritual gift. No one Christian has every gift, but every Christian has at least one spiritual gift.

Paul told the Roman church, "So we, being many, are one body in Christ, and individually members of one another. Having then gifts differing according to the grace that is given to us" (Rom. 12:5-6). Since every Christian has received the grace of God, therefore, every Christian has received a spiritual gift. Peter offered this counsel, "As each one has received a gift, minister it to one another, as good stewards of the manifold grace of God" (1 Peter 4:10).

It doesn't matter who you are, what your IQ is, or how limited your abilities may be, you are a gifted child! You have a ministry in the church that God wants you to do, and it will not be done unless you do it.

Because you have a certain gift you should not be arrogant or proud. Spiritual gifts should not puff you up as they did the Corinthian church, but rather should humble you. You are so important to God that He has placed you in His service and gifted you to do exactly His will.

Your spiritual gift should make you confident of God's calling. No Christian should ever say, "I am of no use to God," or "I'm not needed in the church," or "There is no way God can use me." Every Christian is a minister and every Christian has a ministry. The ministry of the church is to be carried out as individual believers exercise their spiritual gifts in ministering to others. To the extent that you do not exercise your spiritual gift, you hinder the ministry of the total church.

They Are Distributed Independently

We are also told in verse 11 that the Spirit gives these gifts "as He wills." The Holy Spirit decides the gift you are going to have. You do not have any choice in the matter. You cannot determine your spiritual gift any more than your birthplace or the color of your eyes. The Holy Spirit sovereignly distributes these gifts as He wills, because He knows what is best for the body.

Some Christians would like to practice what I call, "cafeteria Christianity." They would like to select their spiritual gifts just as they choose food in a cafeteria. "I'd like some tongues please, but I wouldn't care for any administration." Or, "I'd like a double portion of healing, but I'll pass on the gift of giving." But the Holy Spirit knows what is best, and He gives the gifts accordingly.

Therefore, one Christian should never be jealous of another who has a different gift. Paul had an answer, "For who makes you differ from one another? [obviously, the answer is God] And what do you have that you did not receive? Now if you did indeed receive it, why do you glory as if you had not received it?" (1 Cor. 4:7)

All of us have been gifted differently, but all of us have been gifted perfectly. The Holy Spirit, in His divine wisdom, has given to each of us precisely the gift, or gifts, that will enable us to function most effectively in the body of Christ.

They Are Distributed Intentionally

Why has the Holy Spirit distributed these gifts in such a fashion? Why doesn't the Holy Spirit give every Christian every gift? Or why doesn't He give every Christian the same gift?

Again, these gifts are not given arbitrarily, but with a definite purpose in mind, as we find in verse 7, "But the manifestation of the Spirit is given to each one for the profit of all." The word "profit" literally means "to bring together" or "to join together." God has made us different that He might make us one.

Why are the pieces of a puzzle all different? So they will all fit together. We have different gifts so that we might all fit together in the body of Christ. In fact, Paul uses the very analogy of a body, beginning in verse 12, to illustrate that we are to be joined working together just like the different parts of a body. He uses this analogy to illustrate the purpose of spiritual gifts.

We are to be *different* from one another. "For as the body is one and has many members, but all the members of that one body, being many, are one body, so also is Christ" (v. 12). All parts of my body are important, but they are all different. I thank God that they are. If I had eyes for kidneys, I would be dead. If I had kidneys for eyes, I would be ugly and blind. But I have different bodily parts because each one has a different function.

We live in a society today that is trying to make everyone the same. There is the unisex movement which is trying to eradicate the differences between men and women. There is the Gay Rights' Movement which is trying to convince us that the only difference between homosexuals and heterosexuals is "different sexual preferences." But the more you try to eliminate differences, the more you will only emphasize differences.

There is not only to be a unity, but there is to be a diversity in the church. There is to be a unity in our diversity, but our diversity will strengthen our unity, not weaken it. You are who you are, and I am who I am. I'm gifted the way I'm gifted, and you are gifted the way you're gifted. We are both different and we were meant to be different. We were not meant to be the same.

We are to be *dependent* on one another. It takes every part working together to have a healthy body that will function properly. Every part of my body is dependent on another to do its work.

When I drive I need my eyes to guide the car. I need my

hands to steer it, and I need my feet to drive it. Now my eyes, hands, and feet are not competing with each other, they are completing each other. Every part is needed because each part is dependent on the other.

Spiritual gifts teach us that we really do need each other. That is Paul's whole point in verses 18-23. The eye can do things the foot cannot do and the foot can do things the eye cannot do, but both need the other. There is no such thing as "lone-ranger Christianity." There is no such thing as a Christian who does not need to be in church. You don't have to go to church to be a Christian, but you need to go to be a growing and useful believer.

You may be a foot in the body of Christ, but if you injure a foot you cripple the body. You may be an eye in the body, but if you are missing an eye you will be blind. Just as your body needs every part working together, so does the body of Christ. Everybody is needed.

But not only is every member of the body equally needed, every member is equally important. That is what Paul is telling us in verses 14-18. Some of us are outspoken, others are quiet. Some are dynamic, some are laid back. There are leaders, others are followers. Some of us are noticeable, some are inconspicuous. But we are all equally needed and all equally important. You have a gift. I have a gift. Our gifts are to be exercised together for God's work. That means that *everybody is somebody* in His body.

There is an old parable of some Tools that were having a meeting. Brother Hammer was presiding, but the Tools had decided they no longer wanted Brother Hammer to lead. As a matter of fact, they wanted him kicked out of the Tool Chest because he was rough and always made a lot of noise.

Brother Hammer heatedly responded, "Well, if I have to go, Brother Screw will have to go too, because he is so lazy you have to turn him over and over to get him to do anything."

Brother Screw jumped up and said, "If I have to go, Brother Plane has to go. All the work he ever does is just on the surface. He never gets down to where the deep hard work is."

Brother Plane stood up and replied, "If I have to go so does Mr. Saw. He has so many rough edges that he is always doing things that are very cutting."

Brother Saw jumped to his feet and said, "Well, if I have to go, Mrs. Sandpaper has to go. She is so rough, and she's always rubbing people the wrong way."

The Tools were at one another's throat until the Carpenter from Nazareth took them all to His workbench. Using each tool, He made a pulpit from which to preach the Word of God. Then the Tools discovered that when they were yielded to the hands of the Carpenter, they could be used working together to build something no one tool could alone.

Mr. Hammer addressed the Tools again and said, "It seems to me that when we work together each doing what we were made to do, the Master can use us." Then all the Tools cried out, "Mr. Hammer, you hit the nail right on the head!"

We all need to learn one lesson: It does not matter who gets the credit as long as the job gets done and God gets the glory.

We are to be *devoted* to one another. We are told in verses 24-26, "But God composed the body, having given greater honor to that part which lacks it, that there should be no schism in the body, but that the members should have the same care for one another. And if one member suffers, all the members suffer with it; or if one member is honored, all the members rejoice with it." That is exactly the way a body functions. When I catch a briar in my right hand, my mouth says, "Ouch!" My brain tells my left hand to remove the briar. My tongue then licks my hand and gives it comfort. Then the body is happy again.

When one member hurts, the body hurts, because the many members are one body. We are to be one in sorrow. We are to be one in success. We are to be one in remorse. And we are to be one in rejoicing. For we are all one body.

THE DYNAMIC OF SPIRITUAL GIFTS

We must remember that the dynamic behind spiritual gifts is the Holy Spirit. "One and the same Spirit works all these things"

(v. 11). It is the Holy Spirit who gives you your gift, and He does this at the point of salvation. We are told in verse 13, "For by one Spirit we were all baptized into one body—whether Jews or Greeks, whether slaves or free—and have all been made to drink into one Spirit." When God saved you He placed you into the body of Christ. You were baptized by the Holy Spirit into His body. At that moment He gave you a gift to exercise in that body.

Every Christian has been baptized by the Holy Spirit. This happens at salvation. That is why you never find a command in the Bible to be baptized with the Holy Spirit. There is a command to be filled with the Spirit, because that is a repeatable experience (Eph. 5:18). But we are never commanded to be baptized with the Holy Spirit, because that is a once and for all experience that happens when you are saved.

Likewise, you get your spiritual gift at the moment of salvation. If you are saved you do not need to receive your spiritual gift, you already have it. Christmas comes for every Christian the day he is born again. For it is then that one receives not only the gift of the Holy Spirit, but also the gifts of the Holy Spirit.

We do not need to receive our spiritual gift, we need to discover it and use it for the glory of God. You are not saved until you receive the Holy Spirit. But when you receive the gift of the Spirit, you then receive gifts from the Spirit.

The mark of a Christian's salvation is possession of the Spirit. This same Spirit has given you a spiritual gift (or gifts) for serving Him. God wants to use you. He wants to make you a gifted child. He wants you to work in His body. But God can't use you until you discover your gift(s). In the following chapters you'll learn more about the nature of spiritual gifts so that you might be a faithful, functioning part of His glorious body!

EXPLORING SPIRITUAL GIFTS: PART ONE

We began this section with an *examination* of spiritual gifts. We dealt first with the description of the gifts. We said, first of all, they are *spiritual* gifts. They are gifts given by the Holy Spirit.

They have been given with a purpose. Spiritual gifts are to teach us three lessons. First of all, we learn that we are to be different from one another. We each have a different gift to be exercised in a different way, for a different ministry, with different results because we are indeed different.

Secondly, they teach us that we are to be dependent on one another. No Christian has every gift. But every gift is needed in the body of Christ. Just like a body needs every member, so is every member of the body of Christ needed. We are not to compete with one another; we are to complete one another.

Finally, we learn that we are to be devoted to one another. Spiritual gifts are to be something which unite us and not divide us. The fact that we all have different gifts, and that all the gifts are needed, is a basis for our unity in the Lord.

We come now to the *exploration* of spiritual gifts. We will do this through a detailed analysis (in 1 Corinthians 12) of the major spiritual gifts that are meant to be operative in the body of Christ. As we do, there are three summary principles that we need to remember.

First of all, *every Christian has a particular spiritual gift.* "As each one has received a gift, minister it to one another, as good stewards of the manifold grace of God" (1 Peter 4:10). Every Christian should be interested in spiritual gifts because no one has been left out.

Secondly, *Christians will exercise their gifts in different ways.* We all serve the same God. We all received our gifts from the same Spirit. But because we are all different, we're all going to exercise our gifts in different ways. One person should not be forced into the mold of another. Two preachers may have the gift of prophecy, but they may have two different preaching styles, and two different kinds of ministries.

Finally, *Christians will see different results by the exercise of their particular gifts.* A Christian with the gift of administration will see different results than a person with the gift of mercy. A person with the gift of teaching will bear different fruit than the person with the gift of giving. Our job is to concentrate not on the results of our gifts, but on exercising them effectively for the glory of God. These three crucial principles must be kept in mind as we begin our exploration of spiritual gifts.

THE DIVISION OF SPIRITUAL GIFTS

We are dealing with "the spirituals" (12:1), those things pertaining to the Holy Spirit. Paul has divided the spirituals in three distinct categories. In verse 4 he tells us "there are diversities of gifts." In verse 5 he tells us "there are differences of ministries." In verse 6 he tells us "there are diversities of activities." These are the three major categories under the spirituals: gifts, ministries, and activities.

The Holy Spirit motivates us to serve the Lord along these three lines. They are related one to another, but they are not the same.

Motivational Gifts

Verse 4 deals with grace gifts. There are different diversities of gifts. The word there is *charismaton*, which means gifts of grace.

These gifts represent our basic motivations. These are the gifts that make you do what you do. They moveyou to serve. They are what drive you to express your love and your ministry in the body of Christ. They even determine the way you see a particular situation. You might say that these are the gifts that make your spiritual clock tick.

We are not only saved by grace, we serve by grace. We serve through exercising the particular grace gift that God has given to us. These gifts are found in Romans 12:3-9.

Ministerial Gifts

We are told in verse 5 that there are differences of "ministries." The Greek word for ministry is the one from which we get the word *deacon,* and it literally means to serve. You perform your ministry through your motivation. The ministerial gifts are those opportunities of Christian service which God gives to us so that we might exercise our basic motivational gift. These gifts are found in 1 Corinthians 12:27-31.

Manifestation Gifts

We are told in verse 6, "there are diversities of activities." But then in verse 7 that "the manifestation of the Spirit is given to each one." The word for activities is the Greek word *energeia.* We get the word *energy* from that. This represents the results of our ministry.

You might say that the first category represents the *essence* of the gifts. The second category represents the *expression* of the gifts. And the third category represents the *effects* of the gifts. When we exercise our motivational gifts found in Romans 12, through our ministerial gifts, the Holy Spirit determines what manifestations or what results will benefit the church the most. These gifts are found in 1 Corinthians 12:7-11.

The first category, motivational gifts, are the key to understanding all of the others. These are the grace gifts. That means all of us have at least one grace gift, because all of us have received the grace of God. Romans 12:6 says, "Having then gifts differing according to the grace that is given us, let us use them." Now these gifts that Paul mentions beginning in Romans 12:6, are the grace gifts Paul had in mind in 1 Corinthians 12:4, because the same word for "grace gifts" is used in both places.

Every Christian has one of these seven motivational gifts. The ministry of the church basically takes place through the exercise of these seven spiritual gifts. Each Christian has one of them. You are motivated to serve the Lord through one of these particular gifts. As you discover which gift you possess, and what gifts others possess, you will better be able to understand what makes others tick—the way they react to certain situations, and how they should fit into the body of Christ.

THE DISTINCTION OF SPIRITUAL GIFTS

Seven motivational gifts of grace are listed here for us in Romans 12:3-8. They are the gifts of prophecy, ministry, teaching, exhortation, giving, leadership, and mercy.

As the church exercises each of these gifts, the work of Christ is carried on in a harmonious and productive fashion. Remember the term, motivation. You do what you do, in the way you do it, because you are motivated by your particular spiritual gift.

The Gift of Sermonizing

The first gift is that of prophecy. Paul says, "If it is prophecy, let us prophesy in proportion to our faith" (Rom. 12:6). Now what is the gift of prophecy? A person with the gift of prophecy has the spiritual ability to proclaim God's truth in such an authoritative and powerful fashion that lives are changed, the lost are saved, and Christians are motivated for greater maturity and service.

First Corinthians 14 gives us a detailed look at this gift. First of all, it is a *preferred* gift. We are told, "Pursue love and desire spiritual gifts, but especially that you may prophesy" (1 Cor. 14:1). Paul repeats his exhortation, "Therefore, brethren, desire earnestly to prophesy" (1 Cor. 14:39). Prophecy, that spiritual ability to speak an authoritative word for God, should be a desire of all Christians. In a real sense, prophecy is a superior gift. It is listed first among all of the other seven gifts. This gift has more said about it specifically than any other spiritual gift.

It is a preaching gift. Paul says, "That he who prophesies speaks" (1 Cor. 14:3). The gifts can basically be divided into two categories. There are *speaking* gifts and there are *serving* gifts. The gift of prophecy, along with the gifts of teaching and exhortation, are speaking gifts. A prophet is not primarily a *fore*teller, but a *forth*teller. A prophet is not primarily someone who tells the future, but rather someone who speaks for God. The word prophet comes from two words, the word *pro,* which means "for" and the word *phaneo,* which means, "to speak." It literally means "to speak for."

You do not have to be a preacher or an ordained minister to have the gift of prophecy. I believe that most people who have the gift of prophecy are preachers of the Gospel. But you do not have to be; there are lay people in churches who have the gift of prophecy.

Peter, quoting the Prophet Joel, said, "And it shall come to pass in the last days, says God, that I will pour out of My Spirit on all flesh; your sons and your daughters shall prophesy" (Acts 2:17). In these days both men and women will be speaking in an authoritative fashion for God. Women have the gift of prophecy. In Acts 21:8-9 we are told that Philip the evangelist had four virgin daughters who prophesied. There are some wonderful women teachers today who have the gift of prophecy. They are excellent Bible teachers and can speak a word for God with authority and with power.

It is a powerful gift. In 1 Corinthians 14:3 we are told the effects that prophesying has on the church. It brings edification, exhortation, and comfort. It brings edification; this is a gift that will build you up. A person who can take the Word of God and speak it authoritatively can strengthen your faith. He will strengthen your fellowship. She will strengthen your faithfulness.

But there will also be exhortation. You will not only be built up, you will be fired up. The person with the gift of prophecy has the power to motivate and inspire action. When he or she gets through speaking for God you will be ready to charge hell with a water pistol.

There will also be encouragement. The person with a prophecy gift can take the Bible and use it as a salve to soothe a wounded spirit, a thread to bind a broken heart, and as a handkerchief to dry a wet eye.

It is a productive gift. Paul says in 1 Corinthians 14:24-25, "But if all prophesy, and an unbeliever or an uninformed person comes in, he is convinced by all, he is judged by all. And thus the secrets of his heart are revealed; and so, falling down on his face, he will worship God and report that God is truly among you." Notice what happens when a person with the gift of prophecy authoritatively preaches the Word of God.

First of all, it brings *conviction.* Unbelievers who come to church will be convinced. They will be brought face-to-face with their sin. A person with the gift of prophecy has the special ability to use the Bible as a two-edged sword to pierce people and to discern the thoughts and intents of the heart (Heb. 4:12).

Notice this is not done by logic, reasoning, nor argumentation. It is simply done by preaching the Word of God. A lost man can argue with any preacher, no matter how brilliant the preacher may be, but a lost man cannot argue with the Word of God!

Secondly, the gift of prophecy brings *conversion.* People will want to get right with God. Lost people will be saved. The gift of prophecy always bears evangelistic fruit. All spiritual gifts are to be used evangelistically. Spiritual gifts, if used in the power of the Holy Spirit, will bring evangelistic results. But prophecy especially will bear the fruit of evangelism. One of the marks of authoritative prophecy is that the lost are saved.

Also, the gift brings *consecration.* People will be moved to worship God. That is another outcome of all spiritual gifts, that others might be moved to worship God.

The gift finally will result in *confirmation.* The power and the presence of God will be confirmed in the church and in the community. I don't know of a greater thing that I would want an outsider to say about our church than this: "God is truly among you." Whenever God is in the middle of a church you can be sure two things are happening: The Word is being preached and the lost are being saved.

Finally, prophecy is a protected gift. This gift evidently is very important to the Lord. It is so easily abused that several safeguards have been placed around it to keep its practice in order. The gift is very carefully circumscribed. "Let two or three prophets speak, and let the others judge. But if anything is revealed to another who sits by, let the first keep silent for you can all prophesy one by one, that all may learn and all may be encouraged" (1 Cor. 14:29-31).

No person can get up and speak *ex cathedra*. No one can say, "I am an infallible prophet. You have to take every word I say at face value, regardless of what you think or know. Regardless of what the Scriptures teach, you've got to follow me blindly and believe every single thing that I say." That is what the leader of a cult says. That is not what a person with the gift of prophecy says. This gift is limited by three factors.

It is limited by *investigation.* First Corinthians 14:29 says, "Let two or three prophets speak, and let the others judge." When you hear a preacher, you and particularly those of you who have the gift of prophecy, are to discern the truth of the message. No true prophet is ever threatened by someone evaluating the message according to the Word of God.

We are warned in 1 John 4:1, "Beloved, do not believe every spirit, but test the spirits, whether they are of God; because many false prophets have gone out into the world." All preaching ought to follow three steps. There should be proclamation where the Word is preached. Next should be investigation to check the validity of the sermon. Then, only at that point, should there be appropriation, that is the application of the Word to life.

The gift of prophecy is limited by *invitation.* Paul is concerned about preventing two things that could disrupt both a worship service and a church. First of all, proper practice prevents a stranger from coming in and taking over a worship service, claiming that he or she has a word from the Lord. "And the spirits of the prophets are subject to the prophets" (1 Cor. 14:32).

I remember pastoring my second church while still at seminary. One Sunday morning, fifteen minutes before the worship service, one of my deacons came to me and said, "There is a man outside who needs to see you." He was standing out in front of the church. I went outside. He introduced himself and said, "God has told me that I am to preach today. I have a message just for your church. What time do I speak?"

I looked at him and said, "Sir, I will be glad to let you preach, under one condition. If God tells me to let you preach and if God tells me that He told you to tell me to let you preach, then I will let you preach. But unless God tells me that, you are not going to preach." He did not tell me, and the man didn't preach! It was exactly the kind of situation that Paul wanted to prevent.

This limitation also prevents someone from disrupting the middle of a worship service by saying, "God has told me to say such and such a thing." Verses 30-31 tell us, "But if anything is revealed to another who sits by, let the first keep silent. For you can all prophesy one by one that all may learn, and all may be encouraged."

The pastor is to be in charge of the worship service. As long as the pastor is speaking, no one else is to speak unless receiving permission.

If someone were to stand up in a worship service while I was preaching and begin to speak, I would simply say, "Sit down and be quiet." If this didn't work, the person would be escorted out of the service. My justification is "Let all things be done decently and in order" (1 Cor. 14:40).

Finally, the gift is limited by *inspiration*. "If anyone thinks himself to be a prophet or spiritual, let him acknowledge that the things which I write to you are the commandments of the Lord" (1 Cor. 14:37). All prophecy, all speaking for God, is subject to the Word of God. "The testimony of Jesus is the spirit of prophecy" (Rev. 19:10). Jesus said in John 5:39, "You search the Scriptures . . . and these are they which testify of Me." All prophecy, which is the testimony of Jesus, is limited by the Scripture which testifies of the Lord.

A true prophet will never bring any correction, addition, or subtraction to the Word of God. In fact, Revelation 22:18-19 warns, "For I testify to everyone who hears the words of the prophecy of this book: If anyone adds to these things, God will add to him the plagues that are written in this book; and if anyone takes away from the words of the book of this prophecy, God shall take away his part from the Book of Life, from the holy city, and from the things which are written in this book."

Though we still have the gift of prophecy, we no longer have the office of prophet like some cults teach. We do not need any more prophets giving us a new word from God. We simply need men and women with the gift of prophecy to proclaim the old Word of God.

Prophecy never brings a new revelation. But rather, it always brings a fresh and a clearer application of old revelation. Charles Haddon Spurgeon said, "If what you are preaching is new, it is not true. And if what you are preaching is true, it is not new."

Everyone has been created for the same purpose. That purpose is to glorify God. Now the greatest way to glorify God is to worship Him. The greatest way to worship God is to serve Him. You are to serve God by His grace. Romans 12:6 says, "Having then gifts differing according to the grace that is given to us, let us use them."

Once you are saved you can serve. The way that you serve is the same way you are saved, and that is by grace. Every Christian has received one grace gift. Again, I challenge you to fulfill God's prescription by finding your gift. Because when you are saved by grace and then begin to serve through grace, you will be happy, God will be blessed, the church will be edified, and Jesus will be glorified.

EXPLORING SPIRITUAL GIFTS: PART TWO

Seven is the number representing completeness in the Bible. I don't believe it's coincidental, but rather fundamental that there are seven motivational gifts.

I have given each basic motivational gift a special title. In the last chapter we looked at the first of these gifts, prophecy, which I called the gift of *sermonizing*. In this chapter we'll examine the gifts of ministry, which I call *serving*; teaching, which I call *stabilizing*, and exhortation, which I call *stimulating*. In the next chapter we'll cover the gifts of giving, ruling, and mercy which I call *sharing, supervising,* and *sympathizing*.

THE GIFT OF SERVING

Some have been given the gift of ministry. As Paul says, "Or ministry, let us use it in our ministering" (Rom. 12:7). There are those in the body of Christ who have the gift of service. I would hasten to add that service is a duty that is incumbent upon every Christian, as well as a gift that is especially given to particular believers. Every Christian is a minister, and every Christian has a ministry. Every Christian is to be a servant of the Lord and a servant of the church. But there is a special gift of service.

From the Greek word for ministry we get our word *deacon*. The word deacon comes from a verb which literally means "to serve." Someone with the gift of service has a motivation to demonstrate love to others by meeting their practical needs. The gift of service is the spiritual gift of serving others, especially fellow Christians, in a practical way so as to free them to do other tasks in the body of Christ. I believe this gift may be the backbone of all of the others, for this one especially frees those with other gifts to be used in the service of the church.

The gift of service is a *laboring* gift. Someone with this gift has the gift of work. The best example of this gift is found in the sixth chapter of the Book of Acts.

There was a problem in the early church that needed to be resolved very quickly. Some of the widows were being neglected in the daily distribution of food that was to be given to the hungry and needy. The apostles, rather than forsaking the work that God had called them to do, asked the church to call out seven men to serve tables.

It is interesting to note that these men who were to serve tables, were to be "full of the Holy Spirit and wisdom" (Acts 6:3). Never ever separate spiritual work from secular work. All work is spiritual. These men who were to be involved in food distribution were to be full of the Holy Spirit. An usher who passes an offering plate should be just as filled with the Spirit as a pastor who preaches the Word of God. All service is sanctified service in the eyes of the Lord and is to be done in the power of the Holy Spirit.

There are some people who get things done; they have the gift of ruling or leadership. But there are others who do those things; these people have the gift of service. These people like to roll up their sleeves and work. They like to do things for others.

Robert Frost said, "The world is full of willing people; some are willing to work and the rest are willing to let them." People with the gift of service are willing to work. They have no desire to supervise. They get no joy in telling someone what to do or how to do it. They have a "let me help you" attitude. That is why I call it a laboring gift. It is a roll-up-your-sleeves and get-to-work kind of gift.

It is a *liberating* gift. Those with the gift of service love to do things for others, especially in the body of Christ so that they can free others to do what they have been called to do. Notice in Acts 6:4 that the purpose of deacons was to free the apostles "to prayer and to the ministry of the Word." The primary function of a deacon is to free the pastor more fully for prayer and the preaching of the Word of God.

It is interesting to notice that service and prophecy are closely linked together. One of the primary purposes of the gift of service is to free up the gift of prophecy. Indeed, Peter said, "As each one has received a gift, minister it to one another, as good stewards of the manifold grace of God. If anyone speaks, let him speak as the oracles of God. If anyone ministers, let him do it as with the ability which God supplies, that in all things God may be glorified through Jesus Christ" (1 Peter 4:10-11). One with the service gift can meet the practical needs of one with the prophecy gift, thereby freeing up that person to study and prepare to preach the Word.

We noted earlier that you could divide the seven motivational gifts up into service and speaking gifts. I believe one of the primary purposes of the serving gifts is to free up the speaking ones. Without service there would be very little prophecy in the church.

Suppose I was responsible for turning on the lights and the heat, helping to park cars, greeting the guests, signing the checks, and passing the offering plate. I would scarcely have time to be in the study praying and preparing sermon messages. We should be thankful for those involved in gifts of service and labor which allow others to concentrate on their God-given gift.

Finally, it is a *loving* gift. Those who have the gift of service are willing to work behind the scenes. They are not interested in being on the stage; they just want to make sure the show goes on. They are not out for glory or recognition. Their goal is to help get the job done. They do not serve because they have to, but because they want to.

THE GIFT OF STABILIZING

Paul refers to the gift of teaching in Romans 12:7: "he who teaches in teaching." I call this the gift of stabilizing because it is sound Bible teaching which helps to ground Christians in their faith and faithfulness.

This is an *informative* gift. The spiritual gift of teaching is the ability to study and interpret the Scripture correctly, concisely, and clearly, clarify truth, and communicate Bible teaching that results in spiritual growth and edification. In other words, it is the spiritual ability to make the Bible interesting, informative, and relevant.

There is a difference between prophecy and teaching. Although both are speaking gifts, they are each motivated for different reasons, seek to accomplish different tasks, and usually have very different results. Some preachers have more of a teaching ministry than they do a prophetic ministry. Others have more of a prophetic ministry than they do of a teaching ministry. Certain pastors are more teachers than they are preachers. Others are more preachers than they are teachers.

Teaching Characteristics

There is a basic difference between prophecy and teaching. *Prophecy is primarily aimed at the will, while teaching is primarily aimed at the mind.* Preaching tries to move the will to action, while teaching tries to move the mind to understanding. A preacher will try to set your heart on fire, while a teacher will try to get your mind on track.

It is an *impressive* gift. The classic example of a true teacher is found in Acts 18:24-28, where we discover a silver-tongued Bible teacher by the name of Apollos. I find five characteristics of a person with the gift of teaching in him. First of all, a teacher is *eloquent*. In verse 24 we are told that Apollos was "an eloquent man." A teacher will be eloquent. Now the word eloquent does not necessarily refer to speaking ability. A teacher may not necessarily be a spellbinding speaker, but he or she will be interesting. A teacher knows how to communicate.

Teachers have the ability to make Bible doctrine clear. If you do not understand what a person says, it doesn't matter how beautifully it is said, he or she is a poor teacher. The one who knows it the best can say it the simplest. A good teacher never complicates the simple, but always simplifies the complicated. Jesus was called the master teacher. We are told in the Bible that the children and the common people heard Him gladly.

A person with the gift of teaching is not only eloquent, but *educated.* We are told in verses 24-25 that Apollos was "mighty in the Scriptures," and "had been instructed in the way of the Lord." By educated, I do not necessarily mean in schools. A person need not have more degrees than a thermometer to be a good Bible teacher. The spiritual gift of teaching is different from the natural ability to teach. You may have a Ph.D. in nuclear physics and yet be unable to teach the Word of God. You may be trained to teach in a college classroom, but not gifted to teach in a Sunday School.

The spiritual gift of teaching is more than just the ability to present Bible facts. It is also the ability to change lives. I have known people who had great ability in terms of presenting Bible facts, but their classes were unmoved. They knew how to cook the food, but they could not get anyone to eat it.

A person with the gift of teaching knows the way of the Lord, not just the way of the world. God speaks *through* the teacher because God has spoken *to* the teacher. If you have the gift of teaching you teach not just what you know in your head, but who you know in your heart. A person with a gift of teaching may slay the king's English, but at least he knows the King. That is why you cannot measure a teacher by his vocabulary or by his pedigree.

I agree with that old country farmer who said to a young preacher, "I would rather hear a man say 'I seen' when he has seen something, than to hear a man say 'I have seen' when he ain't seen nothing!"

One with the gift of teaching is also *excited.* We are told in verse 25 that Apollos was "fervent in spirit." The word fervent comes from the Greek word that means "to boil." A real Bible teacher is excited about teaching. It will not be the bland leading the bland. A teacher will be genuinely excited about what God has revealed and will be excited about sharing it with others.

Now that does not necessarily mean that a teacher will be a dynamic speaker, but a person with the gift of teaching will get students excited about the Bible because of a personal excitement about the Word of God. You are not ready to teach or preach the Scriptures until you are excited about your lesson or sermon.

One with the gift of teaching is also *exacting*. We are told about Apollos in verse 25, "He spoke and taught accurately the things of the Lord." A believer with the gift of teaching likes to dig out the facts. The gifted teacher likes to get into a nook with a book and study the Word. She likes to cut the Word of God straight. She wants what she says to be informative and interesting. But as much as possible, she wants it to be infallible. She wants it to be true and accurate.

The spiritually gifted teacher is also *effective*. The result of Apollos' teaching was, "He greatly helped those who had believed through grace" (v. 27). A person with a spiritual gift of teaching has the ability to meet real needs with his teaching. More than just teaching Bible facts, he has the ability to change lives. He can scratch you exactly where you itch. What he says is practical and relevant and meaty and helps you to grow in your Christian life.

The Role of Teaching
The gift of teaching is an *important* gift. It is a vital part of the Great Commission: "Go therefore and make disciples of all the nations, baptizing them in the name of the Father, and of the Son and of the Holy Spirit, teaching them to observe all things that I have commanded you" (Matt. 28:19-20). Teaching is just as important as soul-winning in the life of the church. Indeed, they go together, they cannot and should never be separated.

Jesus gives us a threefold job description for His church. We are to make disciples—that is evangelism. We are to mark disciples—that is baptism. We are to mature disciples—that is teaching. We are to get people to believe in Jesus. We are to get people to belong to Jesus. And we are to get people to be like Jesus.

We need Bible teaching to grow young Christians. Colossians 1:28 gives us the purpose of all Bible teaching: "Him we preach, warning every man and teaching every man in all wisdom, that we may present every man perfect in Christ Jesus." The word *perfect* there literally means "mature." We are to be maturing young Christians through teaching the Scriptures.

We not only need Bible teaching to grow young Christians, we need Bible teaching to guide all Christians. The best way I know to grow in the Lord and to mature in the faith is to get into a good Bible study class under a good teacher. That is how young Christians in the early church grew. In Acts 2:41-42 we are told, "Then those who gladly received his word were baptized . . . and they continued steadfastly in the apostles' doctrine and fellowship." That is exactly what you get in a good Bible study class. You get both doctrine and fellowship, necessary ingredients for growth.

THE GIFT OF STIMULATING

In Romans 12:8 we are told of the gift of exhortation. This is a very beautiful and fascinating gift. First of all, it is a *noble* gift. Exhortation is the spiritual ability to stimulate and motivate others to believe, obey, and serve God, particularly in difficult times. The gift of exhortation is the gift of encouragement. Such a person is like a spiritual cheerleader with the ability to rally the troops and to spur them on to greater heights for God's glory.

The Greek word for exhortation is the word *parakalew*. It comes from two words, one meaning "along side of" and the other meaning "to call." So it literally means to "call along side of." This is the root of the Greek word *paraclete*, which is the name Jesus gave to the Holy Spirit. The real ministry of the Holy Spirit is to exhort and encourage us on for God. You are never more like the Holy Spirit and never more in tune with His ministry than when you are exhorting the brethren. An exhorter can turn a quitter into a hitter. He can turn a shirker into a worker. She can turn a pessimist into an optimist.

An exhorter can inspire others with renewed courage, spirit, and hope with a ministry of affirmation and appreciation. It is important to remember the distinction between appreciation and affirmation. We appreciate what a person does, but we affirm who a person is. Now appreciation comes and goes because it is usually related to someone's accomplishments, but affirmation goes right to the heart of a person because it is directed to the individual. The person with the gift of exhortation has that ability to make you feel good about yourself. Such a person uplifts, inspires, motivates, and makes you better just by being around you.

It is a *nurturing* gift. An exhorter may encourage and admonish you in different ways that will meet varied needs. But the result will always be to build you up and to make you better.

The gift of exhortation may be expressed in different ways. At times it may be a ministry of continuation. In Acts 11:22-23 we are told, "Then news of these things came to the ears of the church in Jerusalem, and they sent out Barnabas to go as far as Antioch. When he came and had seen the grace of God, he was glad, and encouraged them all that with purpose of heart they should continue with the Lord."

Barnabas was simply encouraging the brethren to continue on with the Lord. He was encouraging them to keep on keeping on. Someone with the gift of exhortation can inspire you to keep on walking with the Lord. He or she knows how to challenge others to do their best and to keep on doing their best for Christ.

At times exhortation will be seen in a ministry of confirmation. For example, in Acts 14:21-22 we are told, "And when they had preached the Gospel to that city and made many disciples, they returned to Lystra, Iconium, and Antioch, strengthening the souls of the disciples, exhorting them to continue in the faith, and saying, 'We must through tribulations enter the kingdom of God.' "

An exhorter is a pillar of strength in difficult times. He knows how to motivate the tough to get going when the going gets tough. She knows how to throw a life preserver of faith to the believer drowning in a sea of doubt.

At times, it will take on a ministry of consolation. In Acts 16:40 we are told, "So they went out of the prison and entered the house of Lydia; and when they had seen the brethren, they encouraged them and departed." Paul and Silas had been in jail, and it looked as if their lives were going to end. The saints were really depressed. After they were released from prison they went and comforted the brethren.

Those with the gift of exhortation have the ability to soothe hurt feelings and dry wet eyes. I believe counselors have the gift of exhortation. Many musicians have this particular gift, the ability through music to comfort, confirm, and to console the brethren.

At times exhortation will take on a ministry of confrontation. In Philippians 4:2 we are told that Paul implored Euodia and Syntyche "to be of the same mind in the Lord." Here were two women in the church who could not get along. They were fighting and Paul had to confront them and exhort them to come together as one in the Lord. An exhorter sometimes has to be firm. He sometimes has to take the role of a peacemaker.

Exhortation is a *neglected* gift. I know of no ministry so neglected in the church today as that of encouragement. It is so easy to find discouragement and so difficult to find encouragement. You can find a discouraging word almost anywhere, even "out on the range."

There are so many discouraging words to be heard, even around the church. Every church has a "cold-water committee." They are always ready to tell you why something won't work. They are always ready to point out how some program went wrong. Talk about things they don't like—and they're readily available. They seem to talk louder and longer than the encouragers in the church, which leads me to a final conclusion.

Exhortation is a *needed* gift. I do not know of a ministry more needed than the ministry of encouragement and exhortation. Everybody needs encouragement. No matter how well things may be going, no matter how well someone may look on the outside, everyone can use some encouragement. In fact, exhortation is so important that the whole church is to be involved in this ministry.

In Hebrews 10:24-25 we are told, "Let us consider one another in order to stir up love and good works, not forsaking the assembling of ourselves together, as is the matter of some, but exhorting one another, and so much the more as you see the Day approaching." We are to come to church every Sunday so that we might exhort one another. You see, we do not need to be knocking each other down. The world, the flesh, and the devil will do enough of that. We need to be picking each other up.

The church ought to be a place where encouragement rules the day. How we need the gift of exhortation. We need to encourage people when they don't need it, and not wait until they do need it. If we wait too long often our encouragement is too late. We don't need to wait until something good happens to say an encouraging word.

I recall reading about some parents who were worried sick about their eight-year-old boy. For eight years their son had never spoken a word to anybody. One day the boy looked up at breakfast and said, "Could I please have a little more sugar on my oatmeal?"

The parents jumped for joy. They were hysterical with glee. They said, "You spoke; you said something. Tell us, why have you waited all these years to say something?"

The boy just shrugged his shoulders and said, "Well, up until now everything's been okay."

Don't wait until things are not okay. Give that word of encouragement today. *God's prescription for a healthy Christian* always includes a liberal dose of encouragement.

EXPLORING SPIRITUAL GIFTS: PART THREE

N I N E

Giving, leadership, mercy—where would the church be without these motivational gifts? The final three gifts are crucial to developing healthy Christians and maintaining healthy local church bodies. The first gift we are going to examine is sadly neglected, the second is sorely needed, and the final one is surely necessary.

The gift of giving is sadly neglected. There are people in the church that God wants to be reservoirs of blessing, but who have instead become dams of hoarded wealth.

The gift of leadership is sorely needed. We have a saying among our church staff, "Everything rises and falls on leadership." We need more leaders in our churches, people who are committed to seeing that God's work gets done correctly.

The gift of mercy is surely necessary. There are people everywhere who are hurting, lonely, ill, grieving, depressed, and discouraged who need someone to hurt with them and to personally minister to them and meet their needs.

THE GIFT OF SHARING

Paul speaks next of the person with the gift of giving, "He who gives, with liberality" (Rom. 12:8). It is rather strange to see giving as a spiritual gift, for we all know that giving is something that every Christian should do. Even though some people have the gift of giving, we all ought to give. Because even though *some* have the *gift* of giving, *all* Christians have the *grace* of giving.

Paul in writing to the Corinthians said, "But as you abound in everything—in faith, in speech, in knowledge, in all diligence, and in your love for us—see that you abound in this grace also" (2 Cor. 8:7). One can see from the context that Paul was talking about the grace of giving. Not all have the gift of giving, but all have the grace of giving. Every Christian is commanded to give. We see that over and over in the Word of God.

Jesus taught, "Freely you have received, freely give" (Matt. 10:8) and "Give, and it will be given to you" (Luke 6:38). In Acts 20:35 we are reminded that Jesus said, "It is more blessed to give than to receive." We are told in 2 Corinthians 9:7, "So let each one give as he purposes in his heart." Though every Christian is commanded to give, there are those who actually have the gift of giving. I believe a person with the gift of giving is marked by three characteristics.

The gift of giving is one of *sensitivity*. The word *give* literally means "to share with," or "to give a share of." It is the gift of sharing.

The gift of giving could be defined as the capacity to give liberally to meet the needs of others with no ulterior motive, and with the understanding that all wealth is a gift from God and is to be used for His glory.

The gift of giving is the ability to become a channel of financial and material blessings to others who have need, so that the Word of God is expanded and God is glorified.

People with the gift of giving have sensitivity. They have the ability to recognize when someone is in need. But they also have the motivation and the capacity to meet that need. They don't just pray for those in need, but they desire to be an answer to their own prayers.

It is also a gift of *sensibility*. A person with the gift of giving has the ability to accumulate wealth. It just makes sense that if a person has the gift of giving he also has the gift of getting. There are some people who have the gift of making money. Everything they touch turns to gold. They have "the Midas touch."

It is important for those who have the ability to accumulate wealth to realize that it is a gift from God. We are told in Deuteronomy 8:18, "And you shall remember the Lord your God, for it is He who gives you power to get wealth." Some people think they are wealthy because they know how to wheel and deal. They are puffed up with pride from their prosperity. But, if you have the ability to get wealth it is only because God gave it to you.

Now all Christians are not rich. All Christians are blessed, but not all are rich. But there are some Christians who are rich, prosperous, and blessed. I believe that every rich, prosperous Christian has the gift of giving.

But have you noticed that there are very few wealthy Christians who are really on fire for God? Do you know why I believe that is true? I believe many Christians have learned how to get, but they have not learned how to give. They are always getting, but never giving. If you ever get into the posture of being a getting Christian without being a giving Christian, your life of faith will wither and die on the vine.

There are two seas in Palestine. Both seas are fed by the Jordan River. One sea is fresh, brimming and teeming with life. Fish are in it, splashes of green adorn its banks, and trees spread their branches over it, stretching out their thirsty roots to sip of its healing waters.

But the other sea has no life in it at all. No fish can live in it. No man can drink it for the water is foul and putrid. Yet, both are fed by the Jordan River. What is the difference? Well, the Sea of Galilee receives water from the Jordan, but it also gives. For every drop of water that flows into it, another drop flows out. But the other sea hoards its water. For every drop it gets, it keeps. The Sea of Galilee gives and lives. The other sea gets and keeps. It is called the Dead Sea.

I know a lot of dead-sea Christians. They are always getting, but never giving. They are always accumulating, but never distributing.

Those with the gift of giving have the ability to assess wealth. They know how to make wise investments and to recognize a good deal. Good deals are drawn to them like iron to a magnet. They know how to get the best return on their money.

They also have the ability to administrate well. They know how to put their money where it is most needed, and where it may be best used. Now they are not an easy touch. A spiritual sixth sense helps them to determine whether a person or a cause is worthy of their giving.

Also, it is a gift of *sincerity*. Those who give, do so "with liberality." This word refers to a blanket without a wrinkle or a fold that is completely laid out, where nothing is hidden. A person with the gift of giving gives with no ulterior motive, no hidden agenda.

Different people give for different reasons. Some people give out of *guilt*. They give to God's work because they would feel bad if they didn't. Some people give out of *greed*. They give to get. They think, "I'm going to give because if I do God is going to give back to me." Now it pays to give, but if you give because it pays, it won't pay. Some people give to get a tax break. There is nothing wrong with the tax break, but it is a very poor motive. Some people give out of *glory*. They give so they can brag about it. They are proud when they put their offering in the public plate.

But the only reason we ought to give is out of *gratitude*. We ought to be grateful that God has given to us and grateful that we in turn can give to Him.

God is not just interested in what we give; He is also interested in why we give. Some people look at their tithe in the same way that they look at their tax. They don't give their tithe, they pay it. They give their tax because the government requires it, and they give their tithe because God requires it. God does require the tithe. But there is as much difference between your tithe and your tax as there is between God and the government.

The government does not care why you pay your taxes. If you

pay your taxes because you are patriotic and want to be a good citizen loving mom, country, and apple pie, that is fine with the government. Or if you pay your taxes, kicking, fighting, and screaming all the way to the post office, that is fine with the government too. They just want your tax.

But God is not only interested in the measure of your giving, He is interested in the motive of your giving. If you give to God out of greed, guilt, or glory, God writes a big "0" over your account. "God loves a cheerful giver" (2 Cor. 9:7). A person with the gift of giving gives just to please the Lord.

THE GIFT OF SUPERVISING

Now we turn to the gift of leading, "He who leads, with diligence" (Rom. 12:8). You have heard people referred to as "born leaders." I prefer "born-again leaders," those who have the gift of leading, ruling, and supervising. Those who have the gift of leading will be marked by three traits:

They will have a sense of *direction*. The word *lead* literally means "to stand in front of," or "to stand before." The gift of leadership is the ability to mobilize and motivate a group of people to accomplish a common task and to achieve a common goal. It is the spiritual ability to evaluate, coordinate, and administrate spiritual matters in an orderly way, so that common goals are achieved in the most productive fashion possible.

People with the gift of leadership have a sense of direction. They will be visionary types. They can see the big picture. They can see the puzzle before all of the pieces have been put together. But then they can mobilize and motivate people to put that puzzle together. This is a gift that is sorely needed in our churches today.

We have heard so often that there are "too many chiefs and not enough Indians." I believe that is true in many situations. But I don't believe that is so true in the church. I believe in the church we do not have enough true chiefs. We may have a few people who think they are chiefs who really need to be Indians, but I'm afraid we have too many Indians who need to step forward and become chiefs. We have people today with the gift of leadership who are sitting back and refusing to take their positions in the church, and the work of God is suffering because of it.

I want to repeat: *Everything rises and falls on leadership.* Whenever anything great is accomplished for the kingdom of God, you will always find great leadership. But leadership also rises and falls on followership.

If there are those who are called to lead, that means the rest of us are called to follow. That is why the Bible says, "Obey those who rule over you, and be submissive, for they watch out for your souls, as those who must give account" (Heb. 13:17). Just as a pastor is going to have to give an account as to how a church is led, so the church is going to have to give an account as to how it follows the pastor. God gives a sense of direction to those with the gift of leadership, and then He expects others to get in line and make that vision a reality.

A person with a gift of leadership also has a sense of *delegation.* Leaders do not have to have their fingers in every piece of the pie. They realize that it is better to get ten people to work than it is to do the work of ten people.

Leaders are not afraid to let others have responsibility. They are not afraid to let others get glory and credit for a job well done. As a matter of fact, they don't care who gets the credit as long as the job is accomplished.

In some ways this is just the opposite of the gift of service. Someone with the gift of service is frequently a poor delegator. A servant doesn't want to delegate work, but wants to do work. That is why the gifts of service and leadership are so complementary. The leader knows how to allow the servant to do a job without feeling personally threatened.

One gifted with leadership has a sense of *determination.* The one who leads is to lead "with diligence." Diligence literally means "determination." Leaders must make a determined effort. A leader is not a quitter, and a quitter is not a leader. A leader has a "stick-to-it" attitude.

Leaders ought to have tender hearts, but tough hides. They

can take the heat. Leaders can handle criticism. They can withstand opposition. ey know how to weather the storm.

I read somewhere of some men at sea who were in the midst of a violent storm on an old ship. The ship was quite a leaky vessel, and it had long ago seen its best years. The boiler on the ship was very weak and looked like it might explode at any moment.

One passenger on the ship came to the captain and said, "What's going to happen to us in this storm on a boat like this?"

The captain thought about the leaky condition and the weakness of that boiler, and then responded, "Well, we may go down, or we may go up, but either way we're going on."

That is the mark of a leader. Whether you go down or whether you go up, your attitude is we are going on, we are moving forward.

THE GIFT OF SYMPATHIZING

Paul speaks finally of showing "mercy with cheerfulness" (Rom. 12:8). Everyone is to be merciful whether he has the gift of mercy or not. Jesus said, "Blessed are the merciful, for they shall obtain mercy" (Matt. 5:7). But there are those in the body of Christ who have the gift of mercy.

People with the gift of mercy know how to *relate to the brokenness of others*. The word *sympathy* literally means "to feel with." That is the gift of mercy. That is the gift of sympathetic service.

The gift of mercy is the ability to feel the hurt and the heartache of others and then to share because you care. The person with the gift of mercy knows how to sympathize and empathize with the hurting and the sorrowful.

It is the ability to experience sympathy for the suffering and the needy, and to express that sympathy in a practical way which brings encouragement and comfort to those in need.

There are certain people who know how to weep when you weep. They know how to hurt when you hurt. It seems as if they have the ability to take the threads of your heart and the threads of their heart and knit them together as one. They have the ability to bear and share the burdens of others in an understanding way.

I heard a story once about a farmer who had some puppies for sale. He made a sign advertising the pups and nailed it to a post on the edge of his yard. As he was nailing the sign to the post he felt a tug on his overalls and looked down to see a little boy with a big grin and something in his hand.

"Mister," he said, "I want to buy one of your puppies."

The farmer replied, "These puppies come from fine parents and cost a great deal of money."

The boy dropped his head for a moment and then looked back up at the farmer and said, "I've got thirty-nine cents. Is that enough to take a look?"

"Sure," said the farmer, and with that he whistled and called out, "Dolly, come here, Dolly."

Out from the doghouse and down the ramp ran Dolly, followed by four little balls of fur. The little boy's eyes lighted up with glee. Then out from the doghouse came another little furry ball, but this one was much smaller. Down the ramp it slipped in a feeble attempt to catch up with the others. It hobbled, rather than ran, because it was born with its two hind legs very badly deformed. The little boy looked at the puppy and said, "I want that puppy."

The farmer knelt down and said, "Son, you don't want that puppy. He will never be able to run and play like the other little dogs."

When he said that, the little boy reached down and slowly pulled up one leg of his pants. He revealed a steel brace running down both sides of his leg, attached to a specially made shoe. He looked up at the farmer and said, "Mister, I'll never be able to run with the other boys either, and that little puppy will need somebody who understands."

That is the gift of mercy, the ability to relate to the brokenness of others.

People with this gift know how to *relieve the burdens of others.*

We are told of a young lady with this gift in Acts 9:36: "At Joppa, there was a certain disciple named Tabitha, which is translated Dorcas. This woman was full of good works an charitable deeds which she did." The phrase, "charitable deeds," literally translated would be "mercy deeds." She had the gift not just to feel sorry for the down and out, but to minister to them. A person with the gift of mercy not only feels compassion for the needy, but picks the down up and brings the out in.

The Good Samaritan had this gift. A man had been beaten, robbed, and left for dead. He was lying in the dirt, covered with his own blood, broken, and battered. But the Good Samaritan came along, knelt down in the dirt, cleansed his wounds, bound him up, and took him to an inn and paid for all of his care.

People who have this gift love to visit hospitals. They love to hold the hands of the sick. They love to visit jails. Mercy givers enjoy going to nursing homes and visiting with the shut-ins and the elderly. They have a gift and a desire to minister to the needs of others.

There is a difference between the gifts of mercy and service. The gift of service is directed primarily to Christian workers, so those workers may be relieved to do something else for the body of Christ. But the gift of mercy is directed to the distressed, whether they are churched or unchurched. It is a gift directed to the unfortunate and forgotten, those with tremendous physical needs. It helps those who may never be able to return that help.

Finally, these gifted people know how to *release blessings to others.* Those who exercise this gift, we are told, do so "with cheerfulness." They do what they do not because it is a duty, but because it is a blessing. Everywhere they go they leave behind the aroma of joy and the fragrance of gladness.

Thinking about these last three gifts, I cannot help but think how they were all so beautifully combined in the Lord Jesus Christ. Jesus came from heaven so that He might lead us back to heaven. Jesus can *lead* us to heaven because He has *given* us *mercy* at the Cross. If you will accept the *mercy* that Jesus has *given* to you at the Cross He will *lead* you to a healthy Christian life.

UNDERSTANDING THE MANIFESTATION GIFTS

Having just completed our study of the seven basic motivational gifts found in Romans 12:6-8, I think it would be helpful if we were reminded of several facts. First of all, every Christian has one of these basic gifts as his or her primary gift. As the gift is exercised in the body of Christ, it will be fulfilling a primary ministry in the church. However, as a person exercises his or her primary gift, one of the other gifts may also be exercised in a secondary fashion.

For example, someone with the gift of teaching may, while teaching, exercise the gift of exhortation. Or someone who has the gift of service, may in that service also exercise the gift of mercy. Or someone who has the prophetic gift may in preaching exercise the gift of leadership. Someone may be led to do something God wants done through hearing the message.

Furthermore, these seven basic motivational gifts will have different results or manifestations in the body of Christ. These various manifestational gifts are found in 1 Corinthians 12:8-10, where we'll be focusing in this chapter. For example, a person with the gift of exhortation may be given a word of knowledge about a certain situation to encourage a brother in Christ.

Someone with the gift of mercy, who is ministering to the sick, may be used by God to bring about healing. Someone practicing the gift of prophecy may be given the ability to speak in a foreign language so as to communicate the Gospel in a foreign land. Clearly, there is a strong relationship between the ministerial gifts we have just studied and the motivational gifts we are going to examine. The ministerial gifts will find their effects and results in these motivational gifts.

I have divided these nine manifestation gifts into three basic categories. Three of the gifts I group under the category of wisdom. Two of them I call gifts of worship. And the final four I call gifts of wonders.

THE GIFTS OF WISDOM

Wisdom gifts are those through which God supernaturally imparts insight into the Scripture or into certain situations so that the Word of God may be applied, the will of God may be perceived, and the work of God may be continued.

The Gift of the Word of Wisdom

Paul says in verse 8, "To one is given the word of wisdom through the Spirit." To understand this gift we must first define wisdom. Wisdom is not just knowing the ways of the world. It is not just being a cunning or clever person.

Wisdom is not common sense. There are many people who have a lot of common sense, but they are only wise in the ways of the world. Benjamin Franklin was a very astute and wise man in many ways, but he did not have divine wisdom.

Wisdom is not just education. You may have a Ph.D., but if you don't believe in God, the Bible calls you a fool (Ps. 14:1). As a matter of fact, you may have little education and still be very wise. Dwight L. Moody didn't even finish grammar school, but he was a very wise man indeed, for wisdom is more than just worldly insight.

True wisdom is supernatural in origin. The Bible says in James 1:5, "If any of you lacks wisdom, let him ask of God, who gives to all liberally and without reproach, and it will be given to him." You can get knowledge in a book. You can get an education in a school. But you can only get true wisdom from God.

A word of wisdom is a special, spiritual insight into the ways of God and the Word of God, that gives one the ability to see a situation from His point of view. It is the ability to see things through the eyes of God as He sees them.

For example, I have spoken to people who have given me advice in a certain situation and helped me to see it from a perspective that I had never dreamed. It was almost as if God was speaking through that person giving me a divine insight into an action I needed to take, or giving me some direction for a problem. That is the gift of the word of wisdom.

The Gift of the Word of Knowledge

"To another, the word of knowledge through the same Spirit" (v. 8). Notice carefully that this is the gift of the *word* of knowledge, not the gift of knowledge. No one knows everything. This is not the kind of knowledge that comes from a book. You do not study to achieve and receive this kind of knowledge.

A word of knowledge is when God reveals something to you that you could not know about a particular situation unless He had revealed it to you. It is a special word of insight into a particular situation that may reveal a hidden motive or a future action. There are several examples of this in the Scriptures.

The classic example is found in Acts 5. There was a couple named Ananias and Sapphira who had sold some possessions and brought some of the money to give to the church, but not all of it. They claimed to have given everything that they had to the church. "But Peter said, 'Ananias, why has Satan filled your heart to lie to the Holy Spirit and keep back part of the price of the land for yourself?' " (Acts 5:3) How in the world did Peter know that Ananias had lied? He had no way of knowing except that God revealed it to him through a word of knowledge.

Another example is found in Acts 27 where Paul was on a ship in the middle of a great storm. The storm was so severe that the men on board decided to jump ship in hope of saving their lives. But Paul said, according to Acts 27:22-24, "Now I urge you to take heart, for there will be no loss of life among you, but only of the ship. For there stood by me this night an angel of the God to whom I belong and whom I serve, saying, 'Do not be afraid, Paul; you must be brought before Caesar; and indeed God has granted you all those who sail with you.' " How did Paul know that if they stayed on board they would be saved? The only way was through a word of knowledge.

I believe that Christian counselors many times are allowed to exercise this gift. Have you ever had someone tell you things about yourself that they had no way of knowing, that you knew they could not have known? At times, God allows people to exercise this gift. He gives them words of knowledge.

I remember preaching in a Starlite Crusade in Mississippi and giving the invitation. About forty people had come forward, and I was about to close the invitation. But all of a sudden I said, "There is someone here tonight who had not even intended to come. Your marriage is on the rocks. Your business is about to go bankrupt. You need to be saved. If no one else comes during this invitation, I want you to come." Several other people came, and I really didn't think anything more about it.

The next Sunday in my church a man came walking down the aisle, took me by the hand and said, "I want to be baptized."

I asked, "When were you saved?"

He said, "At the Starlite Crusade."

I said, "Tell me about it."

He replied, "Pastor, you ought to know. You looked right at me and spoke right to me."

I questioned, "I did?"

He then proceeded to tell me how he had driven by the football stadium that night, not even intending to come to the crusade. He saw the great crowd that was there and decided to pull in out of curiosity. He came up into the stands, heard the message, had decided to leave, and then I looked right at him and told him about his failing marriage. I told him about his business. He was about to file bankruptcy. I told him he had not intended to come, and he really hadn't. Then he said, "After you said those things I was too scared not to get saved!" I take instances like that as a word of knowledge.

The Gift of Discerning of Spirits

"To another, discerning of spirits" (v. 10). I put this in the category with the other two gifts because this is a wisdom gift. It takes divine insight to be able to discern false spirits. The word *discern* comes from a Greek word that literally means "to see through." *It refers to someone who can see through false spirits.* It is almost like having spiritual "X-ray vision."

The devil is a great imitator. He is a great deceiver. This world is filled with demons of deceit. It is filled with false spirits. John warned, "Beloved, do not believe every spirit, but test the spirits, whether they are of God; because many false prophets have gone out into the world" (1 John 4:1).

By this gift you can see whether a person's spirit is genuinely of the Lord. One of the most amazing stories in the Bible is found in Acts 16:16-18. There was a young slave girl who was possessed with a spirit of divination. She began to follow Paul around the city of Philippi saying, "These men are the servants of the Most High God, who proclaim to us the way of salvation" (Acts 16:17). Most any preacher would have been flattered by that kind of a compliment. She did this for many days.

But we are told in verse 18, "But Paul, greatly annoyed, turned and said to the spirit, 'I command you in the name of Jesus Christ to come out of her.' And he came out that very hour."

How did Paul know that this girl had a false spirit? Because even though he was primarily exercising the gift of prophecy, his gift was manifested in the discerning of spirits.

There is a difference between this gift and the word of wisdom. False teaching is discovered by a word of wisdom, a supernatural insight into the Word of God that can discern truth from false doctrine. But false spirits may be judged only by discernment. That is why I call it the gift of wisdom as well.

THE GIFTS OF WORSHIP

I put two gifts, faith and prophecy, under this category. I believe these two are linked very closely together. Any true worship of

God will involve some prophecy because God always speaks in worship. But no worship can take place apart from faith, because "without faith it is impossible to please Him" (Heb. 11:6).

There is a great connection, I believe, between these two gifts. The work of God is expanded through faith. The Word of God is expounded through prophecy.

The Gift of Faith

"To another faith by the same Spirit" (v. 9). Some people especially have the gift of faith. Now all Christians have faith. All believers have what we call saving faith. You cannot be saved apart from faith. "For by grace you have been saved through faith" (Eph. 2:8).

But there is a gift of faith. This is the kind of faith Paul speaks of in 1 Corinthians 13:2, "And though I have all faith so that I could remove mountains." Jesus spoke of mountain-moving faith, "I say to you, if you have faith as a mustard seed, you will say to this mountain, 'Move from here to there,' and it will move; and nothing will be impossible for you" (Matt. 17:20).

In my estimation no man exhibited the gift of faith more greatly than George Mueller. Mueller was a wonderful believer who founded a Christian orphanage. Through faith, and faith alone, he raised over $7 million. He knew how to believe God and get things from Him.

Once Mueller was on a ship headed for Quebec. He had to be in Quebec for an appointment that he absolutely could not miss. But the ship was in a deep fog, had dropped anchor, and was not moving at all.

Mueller went up to the deck to see the captain and said, "Captain, I have got to be in Quebec on Saturday afternoon."

The captain responded, "Sir, it is impossible. With this fog we're going to be here several hours, if not an entire day."

Mueller said, "This fog must be lifted. Would you kneel down and pray with me?"

The captain replied, "Man, are you mad? I never heard of such a thing. Do you know how dense this fog is?"

Mueller said, "My eye is not on the fog, it is on God who

controls every circumstance of my life."

Mueller knelt down and prayed one of the most powerful prayers the captain had ever heard. When he had finished the captain started to kneel down to pray, but Mueller said, "Captain, don't even bother. There is no need for you to pray for two reasons: (1) you do not believe God is going to answer your prayer, and (2) if you will look out the window you will see the fog is already lifted." The captain did, and the fog was gone!

Certain people have this special gift of faith. They can see things others cannot see, and attempt things others will not attempt because they believe God. They trust God, not that He can do something, but that He will do something.

The Gift of Prophecy

We have already discussed this gift. It is the gift of declaring the mind and will of God in an authoritative fashion so that His power is released, lost people are saved, and the church is edified. Now all of the gifts are to have a prophetic function. Every gift is to be used in such a way that we can hear the voice of God. All true preaching will have a prophetic element in it.

But one observation is very important. It is not coincidental that this is the one gift of the seven basic motivational ones that is repeated in this list. I believe it is God's way of pointing out to us the importance of prophecy. Never underestimate the power of Spirit-filled, Bible-drilled, anointed preaching of the Word of God.

Lloyd-George, who was the Prime Minister of Great Britain during World War I, declared, "When the chariot of humanity gets stuck . . . nothing will lift it out except great preaching that goes straight to the mind and heart." How important the gift of prophecy is to us all.

THE GIFTS OF WONDERS

These are the most intriguing and mysterious gifts of all. Some believe that these gifts are no longer in existence today. I have difficulties with that particular view, though I certainly respect it. I believe that rather than throwing the baby out with the bathwater, we simply need to clean up the bathwater! I believe that if we understand exactly what these gifts are; that even though they are normative, they are exceptional; and that they are rarely used except in special situations, many difficulties will be eliminated or at least alleviated.

The Gifts of Healings

"To another, gifts of healings by the same Spirit" (v. 9). It is important to notice that both the words "gift" and "healing" are plural here. I believe this is so for two reasons. First of all, there are different kinds of healings. A doctor may be used by God to bring physical healing. A counselor may be used to bring about emotional healing. And a pastor may be used to bring about spiritual healing.

But I also believe it is plural to illustrate that there is no one gift of healing. There are *gifts of healings.* That is, God at certain times and in certain situations through certain people brings healing to the lives of the sick.

Many times I have been asked the question, "Do you believe God still heals people?" My answer to that is, "Only God can heal people." All healing is divine healing.

Doctors do not heal anybody. They are simply instruments in the hand of a healing God. French surgeon Ambroise Pare, who died in 1590, known as "the first of the moderns," had this saying: "I apply the dressing, but God heals the wound." How true that statement is.

Although I do believe in faith healing, I do not believe in faith healers. God still heals. He sometimes uses the doctor to heal. He may use the prayer of faith to heal. Or He may use other means to heal. There is no one who has the singular gift to heal. Nor is it always God's will to heal.

Paul exercised this gift. There was a man who was sick of a fever and dysentery and Paul prayed, laid on hands, and healed him (Acts 28:8). But we are also told in 2 Timothy 4:20 that Paul left Trophimus sick in Miletus. Now if Paul had a permanent gift of healing he certainly would have healed Trophimus.

He told Timothy to "use a little wine for your stomach's sake" (1 Tim. 5:23). If Paul had the perpetual gift of healing he would have healed his stomach. The fact is that Paul had a thorn in the flesh, but could not even heal himself (2 Cor. 12:7-10).

God still heals, but not always. There are gifts of healings. God heals physically, spiritually, emotionally, sometimes miraculously, always supernaturally, but oftentimes through natural means.

The Gift of Working of Miracles

"To another, the working of miracles" (v. 10). This literally says "the working of powers." This is the gift of working miracles. Our God is a miracle-working God. There are times and places where I believe that God works miracles through human instruments. I for one am afraid to deny the gift of miracles, for I might need one sometime!

If you have no problems with God, you should have no problems with miracles. If God can perform a miracle through a great sea monster swallowing a preacher, as he did in the case of Jonah, you should not have any problem with God at times exercising miracles through His preachers, or for anyone else for that matter.

When it comes to spiritual gifts, whether it be miracles, healings, words of wisdom and knowledge, prophecy, or any other gift, I simply do not want to put God in a box. I am not prepared to tell God what He can and what He cannot do.

A grandmother was reading the story of creation from the Book of Genesis to her four-year-old granddaughter. She told the little girl how God had created the skies, the stars, and the moon; how He had scooped out the oceans, heaped up the mountains, hung the stars in their place, and put the worlds in their orbits. She then asked, "Now, honey, what do you think of that?"

"Oh, I just love it," said the little girl, clapping her hands. "You just never know what God is going to do next!"

You really don't! Our God is a sovereign, supernatural, miracle-working God. We need not be afraid of any gift God has given to His body.

The Gift of Tongues

"To another, different kinds of tongues" (v. 10). Unfortunately, the gift of tongues has become one of the most controversial and divisive issues in many churches. Because of this I will be devoting all of the following chapter to focusing on this topic. Since this gift, and its sister gift, the interpretation of tongues, is going to be covered in detail, we will only deal in a summary fashion with these gifts here. I believe the gift of tongues is the supernatural ability to speak in a foreign language, previously unknown, so that the Gospel may be communicated and people might be saved. There is no evidence that I can find that this is an unknown heavenly tongue that someone may use, for example, in their private prayer life. That may be true, but I do not find that in the Scripture and do not understand that to be the gift.

I believe the gift of tongues is a missionary gift. It is a gift primarily for the foreign mission field, whereby preachers and missionaries are given the supernatural ability to preach and speak in a language previously unknown, so that the listeners can understand and respond to the Gospel.

The Gift of Interpretation of Tongues

"To another, the interpretation of tongues" (v. 10). This gift obviously would be the spiritual ability to translate a message in one language previously unknown into the native language of the one who hears it. This again would be a missionary gift, a gift for one who is involved with those who do not speak one's native language.

YOU MUST REMEMBER THIS

One thing to remember about all gifts, especially these gifts of wonders, is that they are designed not to exalt the one who exercises the gift, but to point others to Jesus Christ. Every miracle performed in the Gospels was designed to bring people to the Saviour. When Jesus performed His very first miracle at the wedding of Cana, John was very careful to tell us, "This beginning of signs Jesus did in Cana of Galilee, and manifested His glory" (John 2:11). Every spiritual gift is intended to point people to the Saviour.

If you have been fascinated by these chapters on spiritual gifts, but you have missed the fascination of knowing Jesus Christ as Lord and Saviour, then your personal fascination is nothing more than spiritual assassination, for you will die without any hope of heaven.

The one gift that is greater than all of these spiritual gifts put together is the gift of eternal life. That is one gift every Christian has and that you must receive if you are going to be saved. "The gift of God is eternal life in Christ Jesus our Lord" (Rom. 6:23). God's prescription begins with receiving the gift of eternal life. When you do this you can sing along with Martin Luther's "A Mighty Fortress Is Our God" that "the Spirit and the gifts are ours."

TONGUES FOR TODAY?

ELEVEN

Dealing with the subject of speaking in tongues is akin to handling spiritual nitroglycerin—one false move and everything can blow up in your face! No biblical subject has caused more consternation, fueled more debates, ignited more argument, or divided more churches, than the subject popularly termed "glossolalia."

A cloud of confusion seems to hover over this entire subject. Many people simply do not know what to think about speaking in tongues.

They are like the man who was walking down a country road with a dazed look on his face, dragging a rope behind him. A man happened to meet up with him and inquired, "Sir, may I help you?" The man said, "Well, I am very confused. I do not know whether I have found a rope, or I have lost my mule."

I believe many people are just that confused over the gift of speaking in tongues.

I want my first words about this subject to be Paul's last words found in 1 Corinthians 14:39-40: "Therefore, brethren, desire earnestly to prophesy, and do not forbid to speak with tongues. Let all things be done decently and in order." On the one hand, I am not going to forbid anyone to speak in tongues. Indeed, I do not believe we ought to forbid the exercise of any spiritual gift as long as it is done legitimately and scripturally. I also simply want all things to be done "decently and in order."

Furthermore, I have no ax to grind. The psalmist of old said, "I am a companion of all those who fear You" (Ps. 119:63). I love anyone who loves Jesus and who serves the Lord regardless of their particular viewpoint on this gift.

I want to also say that I am not opposed to enthusiasm and excitement in worship. I'm not opposed to people verbally affirming the Lord in the church. In fact, a child of God ought to be enthusiastic. The word enthusiasm comes from two Greek words, *en theos*, which literally means "in God." If you are in God, and God is in you, you ought to be enthusiastic.

In fact, the charismatic movement is a reaction to some of the dead formalism we have in many of our churches today. I believe many churches are like the restaurant I read about that had a sign out front that said, "Don't Stand Outside Disgusted, Come In and Get Fed Up." I believe there are a lot of people who are disgusted and fed up with dead religion.

On the highway to holiness there are two ditches on either side. There is the ditch of *formalism* on one side and the ditch of *fanaticism* on the other side. The devil really doesn't care which ditch you fall into. I do not believe we need to fall into either ditch. We simply need to stay on the main road.

I believe Paul used a threefold method to deal with this gift and I am going to follow the same methodology.

DETERMINE THE MEANING OF THE GIFT

Exactly what is the gift of speaking in tongues? What do we mean by "glossolalia"? Is it some form of esoteric, ecstatic, angelic babbling that is known only to God? Or is it something else altogether? Before we can deal with this spiritual gift, we need to define exactly what it is.

The Definition of the Word *Tongue*
The Greek word for tongue is the word *glossa*. This word is used fifty times in the New Testament, sixteen times it refers to a

literal human tongue—that is, the physical organ in the mouth. Once, in Acts 2:3, it is used figuratively to refer to tongues of fire. But the other thirty-three times the word means "language." It refers to a foreign language, an earthly language that is spoken by some group or nation on this earth.

For example, in Revelation 5:9 we read, "And they sang a new song, saying, 'You are worthy to take the scroll, and to open its seals; for You were slain and have redeemed us to God by Your blood out of every tribe and *tongue* and people and nation' " (emphasis mine). Obviously, "tongue" here refers to the languages that are spoken by the different tribes and peoples and nations on the earth.

Again, we read this phrase in Revelation 7:9, "After these things I looked, and behold, a great multitude which no one could number, of all nations, tribes, peoples, and tongues." There again, "tongues" refers to languages spoken by the various tribes and peoples that make up the population of the world.

Again in Revelation we read, "You must prophesy again about many peoples, nations, tongues, and kings" (10:11). Obviously, the word there refers to foreign languages.

Now there are some who say that the gift spoken of in 1 Corinthians 14 is an altogether different gift, that in Corinth they were speaking some sort of an angelic heavenly language. It was an unknown language. There are several reasons why I do not believe that is true.

First of all, the word *unknown* is in italics in the *King James Version* (see 1 Cor. 14:2), which means it really is not in the original. It was inserted as an interpretation by the translator, not as part of the translation itself. It seems very clear in 1 Corinthians 12:10 that he means foreign language.

As we know, there are all kinds of foreign languages. There is Hebrew, Greek, Italian, Spanish, Russian, English, etc. But all of these are simply different kinds of languages.

Furthermore, Paul says, "There are, it may be, so many kinds of languages in the world, and none of them is without significance [obviously referring to foreign languages]. Therefore, if I do not know the meaning of the language, I shall be a foreigner to him who speaks, and he who speaks will be a foreigner to me" (1 Cor. 14:10-11). It seems obvious that Paul there is referring to a foreign language.

Paul then quotes a prophecy in 1 Corinthians 14:21, "In the Law it is written: With men of other tongues and other lips, I will speak to this people; and yet, for all that, they will not hear Me." That is a prophecy taken from Isaiah 28:11-12. Isaiah was prophesying the Assyrian takeover of the Jewish people. His point was that God had tried to speak in the Hebrew language and to get them to repent. But when they refused, God said, "For with stammering lips and another tongue He will speak to this people ... yet they would not hear." The point is that, here, tongues obviously refers to a foreign language.

But there is something else to mention. In 1 Corinthians 12:10 and 14:27-28 Paul speaks of the gift of interpretation of tongues. The word interpret simply means "to translate from one language into another."

For example, in Mark 15:34 we read, "And at the ninth hour Jesus cried out with a loud voice saying, 'Eloi, Eloi, lama sabachtani?' which is translated, 'My God, My God, why have You forsaken Me?' " Now the word "translated" there is the same word for "interpretation" found in 1 Corinthians 14. It simply means to translate from one language into another.

Again, in John 9:7 we read, "And He said to him, 'Go, wash in the pool of Siloam' (which is translated, Sent). So he went and washed, and came back seeing." The word there, "translated" again is the word for interpretation. It refers to one foreign language being translated into another language.

So to summarize, the gift of speaking in tongues is the gift of speaking in a foreign language that is totally unknown to the one who is speaking. Now if that is true, we should find an example of this in the Bible, and we do.

The Demonstration of the Work of Tongues
The first example we have of speaking in tongues is at Pentecost in Acts 2:1-11. The Holy Spirit came upon the disciples and they all began to speak with other tongues. "Now there were

dwelling in Jerusalem Jews, devout men, from every nation under heaven. When this sound occurred, the multitude came together, and were confused because everyone heard them speak in his own language. Then they were all amazed and marveled, saying to one another, 'Look, are not all these who speak Galileans?' " (vv. 5-7)

The Galileans were hillbillies. They were country folk and uneducated. People could not believe that these uneducated people were speaking fluently in their own language, that is, in a foreign language.

Now notice carefully in verse 6, "Everyone heard them speak in his own language." Again in verse 8, "How is it that we hear each in our own language in which we were born?" Then in verse 11 we hear them "speaking in our own tongues the wonderful works of God." These were known languages, not heavenly gibberish or angelic babbling. These were tongues that were understood by other people.

In fact, the miracle is even greater than what you see on the surface. In verses 6 and 8 the word for language is the word from which we get our word *dialect*. These people heard the truth, not only in their own general language, but in their specific "dialects." If you were from Northern Egypt you heard these people say, "God loves you." But if you were from Southern Egypt you heard them say, "God loves ya'll too." But the point is we have an example of speaking in tongues and it was speaking in a foreign language.

Another example is in Acts 10. "While Peter was still speaking these words, the Holy Spirit fell upon all of those who heard the Word. And those of the circumcision who believed were astonished, as many as came with Peter, because the gift of the Holy Spirit had been poured out on the Gentiles also. For they heard them speak with tongues and magnify God" (vv. 44-45). Here again, we have a specific example of someone who spoke in tongues. The question is what do we mean here by tongues. Was this a foreign language? Or was it some kind of angelic babbling?

Peter makes it plain in the next chapter. He was in Jerusalem speaking to some of the leaders, recounting the experience of what had happened with the Gentiles. "And as I began to speak, the Holy Spirit fell upon them, as upon us at the beginning. If therefore God gave them the same gift as He gave us when we believed on the Lord Jesus Christ, who was I that I could withstand God?" (Acts 11:15, 17) Notice it was the same gift. Whether by definition or by demonstration, the gift of speaking in tongues is obviously the gift of speaking in a known foreign language.

DIRECT THE MANAGEMENT OF THE GIFT

I am not denouncing the legitimate, biblical gift of speaking in tongues, and neither did Paul. Paul made that plain, "Do not forbid to speak with tongues" (1 Cor. 14:39). That tells me there is a legitimate, biblical, spiritual gift of tongues. Though we should not denounce the use of the gift, we must direct the management of it. This gift was being grossly misused in the Corinthian church. We know that for two reasons.

There Was Confusion from the Gift

"For God is not the author of confusion but of peace, as in all the churches of the saints" (1 Cor. 14:33). There was confusion in this church. The worship services were bedlam. Rather than praise, there was pandemonium. Their worship services were like Grand Central Station on Monday morning—mass confusion.

Now wherever there is confusion you will find the absence of God. God is not the author of confusion. He is the author of peace. He is the author of order and purpose. The astronomers know that our planets all move like the parts of a watch. As a matter of fact, we set our watches by the stars and by the planets. Look at a snowflake or a butterfly wing under a magnifying glass and you will find perfect symmetry and order. God is a God of order, not a God of confusion.

There is confusion today over this gift. We are confused today for the same reason they were confused 2,000 years ago.

This gift is misunderstood and misused. This gift had been given a place of prominence in the church, when in fact it was a secondary gift.

In the list of spiritual gifts found in 1 Corinthians 12:7-10 it is not coincidental that tongues is last. Again, when the gifts are mentioned in verses 29-30 of that same chapter, the gift of tongues is last. Indeed, when Paul mentions these spectacular gifts such as healings and tongues, he says, "Earnestly desire the best gifts" (1 Cor. 12:31). He lets us know that there are gifts that are far better and more productive than speaking in tongues.

He plainly says that the gift of prophecy is greater than the gift of tongues. "I wish you all spoke with tongues, but even more that you prophesied; for he who prophesies is greater than he who speaks with tongues, unless indeed he interprets, that the church may receive edification" (1 Cor. 14:5).

There are many today, as I am sure there were in the Corinthian church, who say that speaking in tongues is the sign that you have been filled with the Holy Spirit. There are some people who treat you like a second-class citizen in the kingdom of God if you don't speak in tongues. They tell you that you are missing some kind of a second blessing, that you really haven't received the fullness of the Holy Spirit if you do not speak in tongues. That is very interesting in light of the fact that Paul makes it very plain that not everyone will have this gift.

Paul asks, "Are all apostles? Are all prophets? Are all teachers? Are all workers of miracles? Do all have gifts of healing? Do all speak with tongues? Do all interpret?" (1 Cor. 12:29-30) The answer obviously is no. Not everyone is going to have this gift, nor should everyone desire this gift. If you needed to have this gift to have the Holy Spirit, obviously every Christian would have this gift.

But there are those who doggedly hold to the claim that speaking in tongues is a sign to the church that you have received the Holy Spirit. That shows a gross ignorance of what Paul said. For he made it plain that tongues "are for a sign, not to those who believe but to unbelievers" (1 Cor. 14:22). Speaking in tongues is not a sign to the church concerning anything. It is to be a sign to people who are lost, not to those who are saved.

If speaking in tongues is a sign that you have been filled or baptized with the Holy Spirit, then Jesus had real problems, because Jesus never spoke in tongues! But you better not say that He was not filled with the Holy Spirit. One real sign that you have been filled with the Holy Spirit is this: You will be a soul-winner. Look at Acts 4:31, "And when they had prayed, the place where they were assembled together was shaken; and they were all filled with the Holy Spirit, and they spoke the Word of God with boldness."

There Was Conflict Over the Gift

"Brethren, do not be children in understanding; however, in malice be babes, but in understanding be mature" (1 Cor. 14:20). The Corinthians were acting like children. They were at each other's throats over the gift of tongues.

Today there is much conflict over this gift. We have thousands of born-again Christians who love Jesus, who believe the Bible, who want God to be glorified, and who are filled with the Holy Spirit, who won't even have a cup of coffee together because the gift of tongues has become a wall that divides rather than a bridge that unites. There is ridicule on one side and therefore rejection on the other.

The entire theme of 1 Corinthians 12 is this: Spiritual gifts were intended by God to bring harmony, not disharmony; to bring unity, not disunity. They were intended to be a rallying point, not a dividing line. So what was Paul's solution?

There Must Be Control of the Gift

Paul placed some very restrictive safeguards on this gift, not to eliminate it, but to regulate it. First of all, there must be an interpreter if this gift is to be used. "But if there is no interpreter, let him keep silent in church and let him speak to himself and to God" (1 Cor. 14:28). Although speaking in tongues and interpreting or translating those tongues were two different gifts, they were never to be used apart from one another. An interpreter could not exercise the gift unless someone spoke in tongues, and a speaker should not exercise the gift unless there was someone to interpret the tongues.

No one is ever supposed to say anything in church unless it can be understood by everybody. Because otherwise the gift then edifies the speaker rather than the church. That is what Paul meant when he said, "He who speaks in a tongue edifies himself, but he who prophesies edifies the church. I wish you all spoke with tongues, but even more that you prophesied; for he who prophesies is greater than he who speaks with tongues, unless indeed he interprets, that the church may receive edification" (1 Cor. 14:4-5).

The next rule was that no more than three could speak in tongues in any given service. First Corinthians 14:27 says, "If anyone speaks in a tongue, let there be two, or at the most three, each in turn, and let one interpret." Now actually, Paul was advocating that preferably only two speak, but absolutely no more than three.

So often today you go to certain worship services and find everybody breaking out at one time into speaking in tongues. That is certainly unscriptural.

Paul goes on to add that only one at a time should speak in tongues. Again, verse 27 says, "each in turn." They were to do it one at a time. Part of the problem in the Corinthian church was that they were all speaking in tongues at the same time. "Therefore if the whole church comes together in one place, and all speak with tongues, and there come in those who are uninformed or unbelievers, will they not say that you are out of your mind?" (1 Cor. 14:23) Anyone knows that if a group of people begin to speak at the same time you have mass confusion. How much more confusing if you have people speaking in *different* languages at the same time!

Now comes the real kicker. Paul says that under no circumstances are women to speak in tongues, "Let your women keep silent in the churches, for they are not permitted to speak" (1 Cor. 14:34). Now there are those who have taken this verse out of context and said that a woman cannot pray or say anything at all in church. But Paul had just given instructions in chapter 11 for women who pray to have their heads covered. No, the context of the passage here is speaking in tongues.

Paul's point is that women, when it comes to speaking in tongues, are to maintain silence. Perhaps we can infer that in this particular instance some women were grossly abusing this gift. Regardless, neither men nor women should be guilty of disrupting corporate worship, even while exercising their gift.

The final principle is that tongues should never cause disorder. "Let all things be done decently and in order" (1 Cor. 14:40). How is this to be done? Paul makes it plain that all spiritual gifts are to be subject to two authorities: to the Word of God and to the man of God.

"If anyone thinks himself to be a prophet or spiritual, let him acknowledge that the things which I write to you are the commandments of the Lord. But if anyone is ignorant let him be ignorant" (1 Cor. 14:37-38). What Paul taught was that anything that is said or done in the church must be subject to the Scripture. If people are not going to subject themselves to the Word of God they ought to be ignored.

But spiritual gifts are also to be subjected to the authority of the man of God: "And the spirits of the prophets are subject to the prophets" (1 Cor. 14:32). No one should ever get up in the middle of a worship service and speak, in a foreign or a native language, unless he or she has the permission of the person who is over that service—usually the pastor.

It is the pastor's job to maintain order and decorum in a service. No one is to usurp the authority of the pastor in any worship service, even if one believes "God told me to do it." God never tells anyone to disrupt a worship service or to divide a church because He is the author of peace and not confusion.

DESCRIBE THE MINISTRY OF THE GIFT

The legitimate biblical gift of speaking in tongues, that is, speaking in a foreign language by the supernatural power of God, has a threefold ministry as seen in 1 Corinthians 14.

The Ministry of Communication

Every verbal spiritual gift, whether it is prophecy, teaching, exhortation, or speaking in tongues, is to communicate the Word of God. One of the real problems with the heavenly gibberish that is passed off today as speaking in tongues is that it doesn't communicate anything.

There is a wise observation in 1 Corinthians 14:7-8, "Even things without life, whether flute or harp, when they make a sound, unless they make a distinction in the sounds, how will it be known what is piped or played? For if the trumpet makes an uncertain sound, who will prepare himself for battle?" An army is in trouble if it doesn't know whether the bugler is playing taps or reveille!

So Paul goes on to say, "So likewise you, unless you utter by the tongue words easy to understand, how will it be known what is spoken? For you will be speaking into the air" (1 Cor. 14:9). It would be better never to say a word than to say a thousand words that cannot be understood, because the result is confusion rather than communication.

The gift of speaking in tongues is to communicate *for* God, not *to* God. There are some people today who claim to have the gift of tongues, but they use it in their private prayer language. I find no evidence of tongues being used this way in the Bible. In fact we are told, "Even so you, since you are zealous for spiritual gifts, let it be for the edification of the church that you seek to excel" (1 Cor. 14:12).

A gift used in a closet cannot possibly edify the church. As a matter of fact, that is the problem we have in the church. We need to get a lot of spiritual gifts out of the closet and into the pew. There are those who say, "Well, my private prayer language edifies me." Paul said that kind of praying edifies no one, not even the speaker.

"For if I pray in a tongue, my spirit prays, but my understanding is unfruitful. What is the result then? I will pray with the spirit, and I will also pray with the understanding. I will sing with the spirit, and I will also sing with the understanding" (1 Cor. 14:14-15). Paul was saying, "I not only pray with my heart, I pray with my head. I understand what I say when I pray."

Remember again that speaking in tongues is a sign to the unbeliever. Now a private prayer language cannot possibly be a sign to anyone, particularly an unbeliever. I would suggest that if your spiritual gift is of such a nature that you feel like you have to go to a closet to exercise it, you might be best to leave it in the closet.

The Ministry of Confirmation

What did Paul mean when he said that tongues were a sign to unbelievers? (1 Cor. 14:22) His point was simply this: when an unbeliever would hear someone preach the Gospel in his or her own language, knowing full well there was no way that the speaker could have possibly known the language beforehand, it would be a sign to this unbeliever that God was at work.

This is in effect an attention-getting sign. It is a sign to those without Christ that God is speaking through a certain preacher and they are to sit up and take notice. That is exactly what we find again at Pentecost: "So they were all amazed and perplexed, saying to one another, 'Whatever could this mean?' " (Acts 2:11) In other words, they believed that they had seen and heard a miracle. Peter was allowed to preach the Gospel and on that day 3,000 people were saved.

The Ministry of Conversion

Remember, Paul was a missionary. Paul did not use his gift in a closet. I don't believe Paul even used his gift in the church, because he said in 1 Corinthians 14:19, "Yet in the church I would rather speak five words with my understanding, that I might teach others also, than ten thousand words in a tongue." Paul used this gift on the mission field.

As I noted earlier, speaking in tongues is primarily a missionary gift. This was a gift that God gave, and that God gives, so that people around the world can hear the Gospel. As Paul went from country to country and people to people establishing churches, God gave to him a supernatural gift to preach the Gospel in foreign languages so that many might hear and believe.

That is what Paul meant when he said, "I wish you all spoke with tongues" (1 Cor. 14:5). Very few people in that day were bilingual, much less multilingual. One would meet all kinds of foreigners in those days. Paul was saying in effect, "It would be my hope that you could exercise this gift every time you meet foreigners to give them the Gospel in their own language that they might hear, understand, and be saved."

What we all need to remember today is that spiritual gifts are not ends in and of themselves. They are means to an end—the end of preaching the Gospel and seeing people come to Christ. The problem is that many people are more interested in a spectacular spiritual experience than they are in seeing people saved.

Dwight L. Moody was presiding over a service one day when a man stood up in the balcony and said, "Mr. Moody, let me tell you about my mountaintop experience."

Moody replied, "Sir, how many souls have you led to Jesus since you've been on that mountain?"

"Why," he said, "none."

Moody said, "Well, sit down. We don't want to hear about that kind of mountaintop experience." I say "Amen!" to that!

We don't need to major on the gifts. We need to major on the Giver, so that the lost might be saved, the church might be edified, and God might be glorified. When we do this we will be practicing healthy Christianity.

THE

Part   *Four*

WITNESS

OF A

HEALTHY

CHRISTIAN

●

WHEN STEAK BECOMES A STUMBLING BLOCK

Imagine that you are at a neighbor's house and are cooking out on the grill. You are cooking some luscious, thick, juicy T-bone steaks. You have never seen such meat in all of your life.

So you happen to ask your neighbor where he gets this meat. He tells you about a brand-new meat market that has just opened down the street. "Well, how much do you pay for this meat?" you ask.

"Well, I pay one dollar a pound."

"A dollar a pound for T-bone steaks? Why I have to pay five dollars a pound where I shop!"

"Oh," he says, "you ought to go to this new store. I have never seen such cheap meat in all of my life."

So the next day you hustle down to this new meat market to load up on T-bone steaks. You are a little bit suspicious when you drive into the parking lot and see the name of this store: "The Godless Grocer." But you are so interested in steaks for one dollar a pound that you quickly dismiss that concern.

You walk into the store and it is just as your neighbor said. There before you are stacks and stacks of the choicest, thickest, juiciest T-bone steaks you have ever seen. There is a little sign over them that says one dollar a pound. You can hardly believe it. You think you have died and gone to meat heaven!

You get a grocery cart with the intention of loading up. But just before you get to the steaks you notice an even larger sign over them that says, "THIS MEAT HAS BEEN DEDICATED TO IDOLS AND USED IN DEMON WORSHIP."

Now I wonder what you would do? How many of you would say, "There is no such thing as an idol, and it doesn't matter to me whether it has been used in demon worship. It's a good buy. Just because it has been dedicated to some idol does not change the color, taste, or texture. I am going to buy that meat."

I wonder how many of you would have a pricked conscience. You, for some reason, just couldn't take that meat. You would say, "That bothers me; that is tainted meat. It is not ordinary; it is demonic meat. There is something about buying that meat that would bother me. Besides that, I'm afraid that if I bought that meat it could hurt my witness, and so I just will not buy it."

Now you see you could have a real church fight on your hands over some steak. It would be the "bargain hunters" versus the "beef haters."

Incidentally, if you are wondering who is right and who is wrong, the answer is in 1 Corinthians 8:8, "But food does not commend us to God; for neither if we eat are we the better, nor if we do not eat are we the worse." That is, it doesn't matter to God whether you eat it or not. "For the kingdom of God is not food and drink, but righteousness and peace and joy in the Holy Spirit" (Rom. 14:17).

It is fine if you do eat it. It is fine if you don't. You are not any more spiritual if you don't eat it, or any less spiritual if you do. But it does matter to God *if* eating your steak becomes a stumbling block to your brother or sister in Christ.

What is right for you may no longer be right if it would be wrong for someone else, and if it would cause them to stumble in their Christian walk.

THE PROBLEM ADDRESSED

Paul handles this difficult issue in 1 Corinthians 8. We'll be taking a detailed look at his message in this chapter. Paul is responding to another question the Corinthians had asked, obviously about idols. For he says in verse 1, "Now concerning things offered to idols." There were two sources of meat in the ancient world: the regular market (where the prices were higher) and the local temples (where meat from pagan sacrifices was cheaper). The stronger, more mature Christians of the church realized that idols could not contaminate food, so they would save money by buying the cheaper meat from the local temples.

But there were weaker Christians in the church, some who had been saved out of this very pagan worship. They could not understand why their fellow believers would want to have anything to do with meat that had been sacrificed to idols.

The stronger Christians, that is "the bargain hunters," were saying in effect: "We're not tied down to the Law. Where the Spirit of the Lord is, there is liberty. We are free to eat, and you are free not to eat. You don't have to eat meat, but don't stick your nose in our business. If we want to eat meat we're going to, because we have that liberty in Christ. We're not going to let you infringe on our liberty." Paul has to remind these stronger Christians about two important facts that must always be remembered about our Christian liberty.

Liberty Is Restricted by Learning

Paul says to these Christians in verse 1, "We know that we all have knowledge." Paul acknowledges that you cannot have liberty without learning. You cannot have freedom without knowing. Jesus said, "You shall know the truth, and the truth shall make you free" (John 8:32).

These Corinthians were certainly folks with heads full of knowledge. Paul even commended them for being "enriched in . . . all knowledge" (1 Cor. 1:5). Furthermore, they not only had knowledge; they knew that they had knowledge. They knew that there was no such thing as an idol. Since they knew this and that there was only one God, they felt they were free to eat meat that had been sacrificed to these imaginary idols.

Their problem was they had knowledge in their heads, but they did not have love in their hearts. They were "spiritual know-it-alls." Paul pointedly reminds, "If anyone thinks that he knows anything, he knows nothing yet as he ought to know" (v. 2). In other words, the person who knows a lot is really the person who realizes he knows so little.

Their knowledge had them all puffed up (v. 1). They were using their knowledge as a weapon to fight with, rather than a tool to build with. They thought their knowledge gave them the right to do anything that they pleased. That is exactly what is wrong with our world today.

The world thinks that all that we need is knowledge. But what we have failed to realize is that knowledge without love does not solve problems, it creates problems. For example, our knowledge has given us the ability to do something previously unknown to man. It has given us the power to destroy the human race.

General Omar Bradley said, "We know more about war than about peace; more about killing than about living. This is our twentieth century's claim to progress: knowledge of science outstrips capacity for control. We have too many men of science, and too few men of God. The world has achieved brilliance without wisdom, power without conscience. We have become a world of nuclear giants and ethical infants." We are a nation of full heads and empty hearts. We have worldly wisdom from below, but we don't have divine wisdom from above.

Liberty Is Restrained by Love

Paul says that "knowledge puffs up, but love edifies" (1 Cor. 8:1). It is knowledge that gives us liberty, but it is love that enables us to use that liberty properly. All liberty has limits. All rights have restrictions. Liberty is not the freedom to do what you want to do, liberty is the power to do what you ought to do.

Knowledge can tell liberty what it has the freedom to do, but love can give liberty the power to do what it ought to do. Our liberty is not to be used to satisfy us; our liberty and freedom is to be used to satisfy the Lord.

First Peter 2:16 says we are "free, yet not using your liberty as a cloak for vice, but as servants of God." Knowledge knows what is right, but love does what is right.

There are two marks of a good teacher. A good teacher, first of all, knows his or her subject. But it is not enough just to know your subject to be a good teacher. A good teacher not only knows the subject, but loves the students. A knowledgeable teacher can tell students the truth, but a loving teacher can motivate students to learn the truth.

On the one hand, liberty must not become license. That is why we need knowledge. On the other hand, liberty must not become legalism. That is why we need love. But we do need both. Love without knowledge is just sentimentality. Knowledge without love is brutality. But knowledge and love is liberty.

You may know that something is right. These Corinthians knew that there was nothing wrong with eating meat sacrificed to imaginary idols. Verse 4 of chapter 8 says, "Therefore concerning the eating of things offered to idols, we know that an idol is nothing in the world, and that there is no other God but one."

But there may be a weaker brother who does not have that knowledge, as Paul describes in verse 7: "However, there is not in everyone that knowledge; for some, with consciousness of the idol, until now eat it as a thing offered to an idol; and their conscience, being weak, is defiled."

That is, not everybody has the liberty you have, because not everybody knows what you know. So before you exercise your liberty you had better consult, not only your head, but your heart. You must not only let knowledge, but also love, be your guide. In other words, before you act, *consult your Bible* and *consider your brother*. But part of the problem here was that not everybody in Corinth was being that considerate.

THE PRACTICE THAT IS ASSAILED

There were some "stronger Christians" in the Corinthian church who were flaunting their liberty. They were not taking their weaker brother into account. Now suppose a person insists on his liberty in Jesus Christ. Suppose he "demands his rights."

144 + GOD'S PRESCRIPTION FOR A HEALTHY CHRISTIAN

His attitude is, "I am free to do such and such a thing and you can like it or lump it. I'm free to eat, you are free not to eat. I won't laugh at you if you don't eat, and don't you condemn me if I do eat. I'm not going to let you inhibit my rights." There were some Christians, supposedly mature ones, who had just that attitude in the church. Their cry was the cry of this generation, "I know my rights."

You are never more like the world and never less like Jesus than when you demand your rights. Jesus never demanded His rights. In fact, Jesus gave up His rights to become our Saviour.

"Let this mind be in you which was also in Christ Jesus, who being in the form of God, did not consider it robbery to be equal with God, but made Himself of no reputation, taking the form of a servant and coming in the likeness of men. And being found in appearance as a man, He humbled Himself and became obedient to the point of death, even the death of the Cross" (Phil. 2:5-8). It is because Jesus gave up some rights that we now have a right to enter heaven.

No man is an island. When a stronger brother flaunts his liberty before a weaker brother, when he exercises his liberty regardless of how it affects and even hinders a weaker brother, he does great damage to the conscience of that weaker brother.

His Conscience Is Warped
The first thing that happens to a weaker brother is that his conscience "being weak, is defiled" (v. 7). Imagine a weaker brother who feels it is wrong to eat meat sacrificed to idols. But he sees a deacon or Sunday School teacher eat it, so he decides to eat it too. Now at that point his conscience is warped; it becomes defiled or contaminated because he is going to do something that his conscience tells him is wrong. Whenever you do something that your conscience tells you is wrong, you have sinned.

There was a similar problem in the church at Rome and Paul reminded them, "He who doubts is condemned if he eats, because he does not eat from faith; for whatever is not from faith is sin" (Rom. 14:23). When you willfully disobey your conscience you are sinning. Your conscience becomes warped because it can no longer be a trustworthy guide.

His Conscience Is Weakened

Verse 10 states, "For if anyone sees you who have knowledge eating in an idol's temple, will not the conscience of him who is weak be emboldened to eat those things offered to idols?" That is, when an immature believer sees a stronger Christian doing something that he thinks is wrong, his conscience may become bolder to violate the laws of God.

His rationale is: "If this mature Christian can do it, then I can do it too." When a person begins to take that attitude it becomes easier to engage in questionable practices, where otherwise one's conscience would say it is wrong.

His Conscience Is Wounded

We read in verse 12, "But when you thus sin against the brethren, and wound their weak conscience, you sin against Christ." Finally, guilt will catch up to this weaker brother. He will begin to doubt his spirituality and his brother's sincerity. He becomes a man with a wounded conscience. He will lose the assurance of his salvation, the joy of his salvation, and will eventually become a spiritual dropout.

You may be saying, "What in the world does this have to do with the twentieth century? We don't have to worry about eating meat sacrificed to idols." Well, the problem is not still with us, but the principle still holds.

Perhaps one of the best contemporary illustrations is that of alcohol. Even among evangelical Christians, there is a difference of opinion. Some see nothing wrong with the moderate use of alcohol, while others are strongly committed to abstinence. As you'll see in my following example, I believe abstinence to be the proper Christian position.

Let's say you are a Christian who thinks that it is all right to have a social drink. You believe as long as you don't get drunk, there is nothing wrong with taking a drink. You know that the Bible does not specifically say "thou shalt not drink."

A young Christian sees you in a grocery store picking up a six-pack of beer. That young Christian thinks to himself, "That's strange; I always thought that Christians didn't drink and shouldn't drink. But he is a strong Christian and if it is all right for him, I guess it is all right for me." So, he too goes to buy a six-pack of beer. His conscience is bothering him, but he buys it anyway. At that point, his conscience is *warped*.

He gets home. His conscience is really working overtime. He begins to rationalize: "But that other brother is a strong Christian, he loves the Lord, and if he can drink I can drink too." He opens up that beer and drinks it, although his conscience is telling him it is wrong. At that point, his conscience is *weakened*.

But then after he is through drinking his conscience finally gets the better of him. He begins to feel terribly guilty. He says to himself, "I was wrong. But I was not only wrong, that Christian brother was also wrong." This man loses his esteem as a Christian and he loses confidence in his brother. At that point, his conscience is *wounded*.

When that happens, the strong Christian has sinned against his weaker brother. But even more than that, he has sinned against Jesus Christ Himself. Jesus died for that weaker brother, and if Jesus died *for* that weaker brother a mature Christian ought to die *to himself* for that weaker brother.

THE PRINCIPLE THAT IS APPLIED

The conclusion of the matter is found in the final verse of chapter 8, "Therefore, if food makes my brother stumble, I will never again eat meat, lest I make my brother stumble" (v. 13). In effect, Paul was saying if it comes to my personal rights, or my brother's spiritual welfare, I will give way to my brother. Now Paul practiced what he preached.

He Defended His Rights
As we look on to chapter 9, we see that Paul applied this principle to his own life. Paul realized he had rights just like

everybody else and he defends his rights. Look at what he says in 1 Corinthians 9:3, "My defense to those who examine me is this." The word *defense* is a legal term which literally means "to give a defense before a court of law." Paul is defending certain rights that he could exercise if he wanted to.

He begins by defending his *ministerial* rights. "Am I not an apostle? Am I not free? Have I not seen Jesus Christ our Lord? Are you not my work in the Lord? If I am not an apostle to others, yet doubtless I am to you. For you are the seal of my apostleship in the Lord" (vv. 1-2). There were some questions in the Corinthian church as to whether they should obey Paul and submit to his leadership. Paul defended his right to authority and to leadership because he was God's man. He had founded the church and had led many of them to the Lord. He was an apostle of Jesus Christ; he deserved to lead and they were obligated to follow.

He defended his *material* rights. "Do we have no right to eat and drink?" (v. 4) Paul had as much right to enjoy good food and drink as anybody else. He was saying in effect, "If you eat steak, the preacher ought to eat steak."

He defended his *marital* rights. "Do we have no right to take along a believing wife, as do also the other apostles, the brothers of the Lord, and Cephas?" (v. 5) Paul had a right not only to be supported himself, but also to be given enough support for a wife and family. Paul was an itinerant evangelist going from place to place. He felt that if he came to preach a revival, the church should not only pay his hotel bill, but a wife's as well. He had a right to that kind of support.

Paul then defended his *monetary* rights. "Or is it only Barnabas and I who have no right to refrain from working? Who ever goes to war at his own expense? Who plants a vineyard and does not eat of its fruit? Or who tends a flock and does not drink of the milk of the flock?" (vv. 6-7) Now Paul compares a pastor to a soldier, sower, and shepherd. A soldier has a right to be paid by the country he fights for. A sower has a right to take food from the crop that he tends. And a shepherd has a right to take milk from the flock that he leads.

It is right for a preacher to be paid—and to be paid well. He goes on to say in verse 11, "If we have sown spiritual things for you, is it a great thing if we reap your material things?" He then sums up the whole matter, "Even so the Lord has commanded that those who preach the Gospel should live from the Gospel" (v. 14). There is nothing wrong with a man making a living from preaching the Gospel. He ought to be paid.

One old country preacher said to his church, "I want you to know that the Gospel is as free as running water, but somebody is going to pay for the plumbing." If a man preaches the Gospel, he ought to live by the Gospel according to Paul.

He Deferred His Rights

He goes on to point out in verse 15, "But I have used none of these things." Paul had voluntarily deferred and set aside his rights. He realized that he did not have the right to give up his liberty in Christ, but he did have the liberty in Christ to give up his rights.

Yet he had no ulterior motive in letting the Corinthians know what he had done. He goes on to say in verse 15, "Nor have I written these things that it should be done so to me." He was not pushing for a raise. He was not asking for them to put him in the budget. He knew that there were people, particularly lost ones, who might be hindered from being saved if he began to take money at this point in his ministry. He concludes, "It would be better for me to die than that anyone should make my boasting void" (v. 15).

Notice how this principle affected his entire life. He goes on to say in verse 19, "For though I am free from all men, I have made myself a servant to all, that I might win the more." Then in verse 22, "To the weak I became as weak, that I might win the weak. I have become all things to all men, that I might by all means save some." The only thing that mattered to Paul was that the lost be saved. He was willing to give up his rights so that lost people could come to Jesus.

If you are in a church long enough, you can always tell who the real soul-winners are. You can always tell the people who realize what is important and what is not. Soul-winners don't wear their feelings on their sleeves. Soul-winners don't go around trying to cause trouble. They don't puff up and pout when things don't go their way. Do you know why?

They realize that hell is real, souls are lost, the time is short, the opportunity is great, the Father is watching, the Saviour is praying, and the Spirit is working. All they want is for people to be saved and come into the kingdom of God. When believers are correctly focused on lost souls they don't have time to worry about feelings and opinions. There is real liberty when you can focus on others and not on yourself. There can be a true transformation of values where people become more important than your rights, possessions, or buildings.

There was a pastor who one day found some unruly boys in his neighborhood. This man had a way with boys. He gathered them together and got them to come to his church. He began to teach them the Word of God. He brought them into this lovely church parlor where they had some very fine furnishings. There he began to teach them about Jesus Christ.

After awhile, some of the deacons called on the pastor because there was not only a transformation in the boys, but also in the parlor!

They said, "Pastor, what are you going to do about this situation? We can't have these boys in our parlor. We just spent far too much money on making this beautiful for our people."

The pastor responded, "One of these days I'm going to have to face my Lord, and I don't believe He is going to say to me, 'Pastor, what did you do with those buildings that I placed in your hand? Are the walls unstained? Are the carpets clean?' I believe He's going to ask me this question: 'Pastor, what did you do with those boys that I entreated into your care? What about their souls? Did you bring their souls to heaven?' "

For the healthy Christian, that is always the question before him or her. We are never to be stumbling blocks. We are to be stepping stones that many might be saved and come to a knowledge of the truth.

WHAT THE WORLD NEEDS NOW

We all like a good love story—the kind with a happy ending. By and large, we are incurable romantics. It has been said, "Love never goes out of style, and it always seems to be in fashion." Today when most everything traditional has been called old-fashioned, when most every custom has been called outmoded, when most all of our cherished values have been called outdated, love is still in style.

Love is still talked about, thought about, written about, and sung about. Song titles say it all, "What the World Needs Now Is Love Sweet Love," "You're Nobody 'Til Somebody Loves You," and "It's Love That Makes the World Go 'Round." One pundit said, "I don't know whether love makes the world go 'round or not, but it certainly makes the trip worthwhile!"

Love is still alive and well on Planet Earth. Boys and girls are still interested in love, and those who are not soon will be. It is a scientific fact that for the first twelve years of life girls are more interested in love than boys. But then in the next four years boys start catching up. From then on it is "neck and neck."

Life has been defined as "one thing after another" while love has been defined as "two things after each other." Though we sing about it, talk about it, think about it, and read about it, much of this world goes to bed at night starved for real love.

Why is it that people will call these "1-900 love" numbers where they can hear a total stranger tell them how much they are loved, how wonderful they are, and hear some kind of romantic fantasy? Because they are hungry for love. Why is it people go to dating services, willing to meet a total stranger, based on some information in a computer? Because they are hungry for love. The problem is, if you go to the wrong place looking for love, you are likely to find the wrong kind of person as well as the wrong kind of love. You don't always get what you are looking for.

What the world needs now is not "love, sweet love." What the world needs now is God's love. It does not need the love of glamour and glitter, whose glow soon fades away. It needs the love of God and grace, whose radiance never ends. This is the kind of love, the love that lasts, that is spoken of in the most beautiful chapter in the Bible, 1 Corinthians 13.

THE MATCHLESS VALUE OF LOVE

As we walk through 1 Corinthians 13, the biblical "lover's lane," we will discover that there are no substitutes for love. There is nothing that can equal the value of love. Yet there are still some things that people try to substitute for love.

Beautiful Speech

"Though I speak with the tongues of men and of angels, but have not love, I have become as sounding brass, or a clanging cymbal" (v. 1). You may be a great speaker, but that is no substitute for love. No matter how great your oratory, how beautiful your speech, how brilliant your rhetoric, without love you are simply a clanging cymbal. You will just turn people off.

Have you ever been to a cymbal solo? I can assure you it is not very exciting. No matter what you say, nor how you say it, nor how accurate it may be, without love it is just noise. Without love, talk truly is cheap.

I have known preachers who were brilliant in the pulpit. They could preach *on* love, but they had never learned how to preach *in* love. There are many theologians and religion professors who know the words, but they have never learned the music.

Two preachers were talking once, and one said, "I just love to preach to my people." The other pastor replied, "That is wonderful. But I want to ask you a question. Do you love the people to whom you preach?"

You see, great oratory can move a person's emotions. Great rhetoric can move a person's mind. A great speech can move a person's will, but only great love can move a person's heart. Oratory can move one to tears, but only love can move one to Jesus.

I know of a man who only had an eighth-grade education. But this man wanted to be a soul-winner. God had laid a brilliant attorney on his heart. Obeying the Lord, he went to talk to the lawyer about Jesus Christ. But no sooner had he begun when the attorney used his legal training and brilliant mind to turn the man inside out.

The man finally apologized for coming and for taking the attorney's time. He left with tears in his eyes as he said to the lawyer, "I just want you to know that I came because I love you."

Dejected, he went home to his wife and said, "I don't want to be bothered. I don't want to talk to anyone the rest of the day. I just want to go to my room and be left alone; I feel such a failure."

About an hour later, the lawyer came and knocked on the man's door. He told the man's wife he would like to see her husband. She said, "I'm sorry, but he is not seeing anyone today."

"Oh," he said, "I think he will see me. Just tell him who I am."

So the husband allowed the attorney to come into his room. He said, "Why have you come? Have you come to make fun of me? Have you come to argue with me again? You know I cannot argue with you."

The lawyer said, "No, I haven't come to argue with you. I

have come to ask you to tell me how to be saved."

The man replied, "I don't understand. What changed your mind? Every time I tried to tell you about Jesus you came up with an argument that I couldn't answer."

The lawyer said, "Yes, I did. But you came up with an argument that I couldn't answer."

This soul-winner looked at him and said, "What was that?"

The lawyer replied, "When you looked at me and told me you loved me, I couldn't argue with that."

Brilliant Scholarship

"And though I have the gift of prophecy, and understand all mysteries and all knowledge" (v. 2). You may know all of the books of the Bible, you may have memorized thousands of verses, you may be able to read Greek and Hebrew, yet without love it is nothing.

John Wesley, founder of the Methodist movement, said, "all learning without Jesus Christ is just splendid ignorance." You see, it is not what you know, but it is who you love that is going to determine whether or not you go to heaven.

You may have knowledge bursting from your head, but if you do not have love bursting from your heart, you are just a big bust. It is far better to have a right heart than it is to have a right head.

The Pharisees were brilliant theologians; they knew the Law and the Scripture inside out. They could split a theological hair into sixteen equal divisions. But they were condemned because they did not love the Lord Jesus Christ.

Bountiful Success

"Though I have all faith, so that I could remove mountains, but have not love, I am nothing" (v. 2). You may have mountain-moving faith, but if you do not have love, you are just one big molehill. What good is faith that can move mountains, if you don't have enough love to remove malice? I believe God is more interested in how much a person loves than how much a person believes.

Without love, your faith is flawed. Jesus did not say by your great faith shall all men know that you are my disciples. He did not say that if you will go out and move mountains, people will come into the kingdom of God. But Jesus did say, "By this all will know that you are My disciples, if you have love for one another" (John 13:35).

You may have moved mountains in your business to become successful. You may have moved mountains in overcoming a physical disability. You may have moved mountains in building your home and putting your children through school. You may have moved mountains in becoming financially independent. But if you have done it all without love for God, it is absolutely nothing.

Benevolent Sacrifice

"Though I bestow all my goods to feed the poor, and though I give my body to be burned, but have not love, it profits me nothing" (v. 3). You can give without loving, but you cannot love without giving. So often people give things instead of giving themselves. Many parents have failed to realize that cars, money, and clothes are no substitute for love.

I have had parents come to me with rebellious teenagers where the generation gap had become as wide as the Grand Canyon. They would say something like, "I don't understand it. I gave this boy everything he ever wanted." I am always tempted to ask, "But did you give that boy the one thing he really needed?"

In a little Florida town there was a home for unwanted boys. They had very little of this world's goods. But the housemother made it up to them the best way she knew how. She loved and mothered them. She taught them to love the Lord and to say their prayers. She spent time with them. They knew that they were loved.

One day a wealthy woman came by to adopt one of the children. She picked out a cute little boy, and all the rest of the children were happy that the boy was going to have a home.

The woman picked the boy up and asked, "I'm so excited that

you're coming home with me. Do you have a bicycle?" He said, "No ma'am." "Well," she promised, "we're going to buy you one."

"Do you have a pair of roller skates?" He said, "Just an old pair." "Well, we're going to buy you a lovely new pair."

"Tell me son, do you have a radio?" The little boy looked puzzled. "I don't have a radio at all." "Well, don't you worry, we're going to get you one."

The little boy began to look very sad and solemn. The woman asked, "What is the matter, son?" The little boy said, "Ma'am, if that is all that you are going to give me if I come to live with you, I'd rather stay here."

People can live without things, but people cannot live without love.

THE MARVELOUS VIRTUES OF LOVE

There is no quality known to man that can equal that of love. The love that lasts, and the kind of love that the world needs now, is characterized by certain beautiful virtues.

Patience
"Love suffers long" (v. 4). There is one Greek word for the two words "suffers long" which literally means "a long anger." In other words, love has a long fuse. It takes a long time to get real love angry. How our homes need more of this kind of patience! Someone has observed that "happy homes are built with the bricks of patience."

Now though love does not get angry quickly, real love sometimes gets angry. Love that never gets angry is not real love at all. Real love gets angry at sin. A loving parent gets angry at the disobedience of a child. A loving Christian gets angry whenever the name of God is used in vain.

But there is a difference between a righteous anger and a raging anger. Love is God's thermostat that He uses to control the temperature of your temper. Even your anger should be a patient, loving, understanding anger.

Kindness

"Love . . . is kind" (v. 4). Love not only does not get angry quickly, love is also quick to show compassion.

One little girl got down on her knees and prayed, "Dear God, please make all of the bad people good, and all of the good people nice." That is what we need in our churches today. We have many good people in our churches who need to be nice people. They need to learn kindness.

There is a difference between kindness and loving-kindness. One boy said to his mother, "Mother, when you put butter on my bread, that is kindness. But when you put jelly and butter on my bread, that is loving-kindness." Real love is kind.

Sincerity

"Love does not envy" (v. 4). Love is not jealous. Does it bother you if someone else gets the raise? What about when someone else gets the praise? How do you feel if another gets the prize? Does it bother you if somebody else gets the promotion? Real love rejoices when something good happens to someone else.

It is sad to say that the cancer of jealousy eats away at the heart of many churches and pastors. So many pastors are jealous of other pastors. They don't like to see other pastors succeed or other churches grow. One old country preacher hit it on the nose when he said, "Real religion is when you can shout in another man's meeting."

Joseph Parker, who lived in London and preached at the same time as Charles Spurgeon, said, "Could I be jealous of the success of another minister? I would be no minister of Christ myself. His success is mine. To that spirit must we come. Tell me of any church that is crowded with eager thousands, that is the scene of daily triumphs in Christ, and I am a member of that church. Its triumphs are ours. We are not divided householders. We are one great family."

Humility

"Love does not parade itself, is not puffed up" (v. 4). Pride and arrogance will not live in the same house as love. They have probably caused more church fights and divided more church families than anything else in the world.

There are no problems too big to solve, but many times there are people who are too little to solve them. The Bible says you cannot be big-headed and big-hearted at the same time.

I heard about a church who gave a man a medal for being so humble, and then took it away from him the first time he wore it!

Love never flaunts itself, but rather it humbles itself. The key line from the movie *Love Story* went like this: "Love means never having to say you're sorry." That is so dumb it is stupid. Love does not mean never having to say you're sorry when you are wrong. If you truly love your wife, husband, children, or friend then you will be willing to admit when you are wrong and apologize for your mistakes.

Courtesy

"Love . . . does not behave rudely" (v. 5). Love is not rude, nor is it crude. It does not snap and it does not bite. One commentator translated this verse, "Love is tactful in its expression." Love is courteous.

Courtesy has been defined as love in little things. That is a good definition. Isn't it amazing to see how courtesy goes out of a relationship once two people leave the dating stage and get married. I read a cute little poem entitled, "Before and After" that says it perfectly:

> Two lovers walking down
>   the street;
> She trips; he murmurs,
>   "Careful, sweet!"
> Now wed, they tread that
>   self-same street;
> She trips; he growls,
>   "Pick up your feet!"

If your love is stronger for your spouse today than it was

yesterday (and it should be, or else it is weaker), then you should be more courteous, gracious, and kind to him or her than you have ever been before, because love is courteous. In fact, the more the love the greater the courtesy.

Control

"Love . . . does not seek its own, is not provoked" (v. 5). This passage could be translated this way, "Love does not fly off the handle." I do not know of anything that destroys one's Christian witness more than a bad temper.

We have at times glorified the human temper. We have mistaken temper for courage. But the truth is when you cannot control your temper, it is not a sign of strength; it is a sign of weakness.

Henry Drummond, a great preacher of yesteryear, said, "No form of vice, not worldliness, not greed of gold, not drunkenness itself, does more to un-Christianize society than an evil temper." Love is God's water to put out the fire of a hateful temper.

Forgiveness

"Love . . . thinks no evil" (v. 5). The Greek word for this phrase is a bookkeeping term. It literally says, "Love does not keep ledgers on evil." Love does not keep an account of evils done against it. Love doesn't keep a book on the bad things. It does not hold grudges. The beautiful thing about true love is that it has a long fuse, but it also has a short memory.

One man was having marital problems and he went to see his pastor. The pastor said, "What is the problem?" He said, "Pastor, every time my wife loses her temper, she gets historical."

The pastor said, "You mean hysterical?" The man said, "No, she throws every mistake I've ever made up to my face."

True love is not only forgiving, true love is forgetful.

> "The heart is a house
>   Where love should abide;
> But when a grudge fills that house
>   Love takes a ride."

Optimism

"Love . . . does not rejoice in iniquity, but rejoices in the truth; bears all things, believes all things, hopes all things, endures all things" (vv. 6-7). Real love's greatest quality is that it always looks for the good in someone else. It is not negative. Real love does not look over someone's faults, it overlooks them.

Julius Gordon said, "Love is not blind—it sees more, not less. But because it sees more, it is willing to see less."

I heard about a husband that was sick, and his wife called the doctor. The doctor came to the house, took one look at the husband and said, "I don't like the looks of your husband at all." The wife responded, "Well, doctor, I don't either, but he is good to the children." Love always looks for the best.

THE MAJESTIC VICTORY OF LOVE

Because love has a matchless value, and because love has marvelous virtues, love is guaranteed a majestic victory.

Love Is Permanent

"Love never fails" (v. 8). Paul has just told us that love will never disappoint. Now he tells us that love will never disappear.

Love never fails because God never fails and He is love. God is not faith, though you do need faith to believe in God. God is not hope, though there is always hope in God. But "God is love" (1 John 4:8). Because God never fails, love will never fail. Because God will always be, love will always be. Only love can put the spiritual gifts in their proper perspective.

Paul's point is that all of the magnificent spiritual gifts will one day cease, but love will not. When the vision of prophecy has disappeared, when the sound of tongues can no longer be heard, when the taste of knowledge has vanished, the aroma of love will still be in the air.

Love Is Preeminent

"And now abide faith, hope, love, these three; but the greatest of these is love" (v. 13). Faith, hope, and love are three of the greatest spiritual qualities a person can ever have. "Without faith, it is impossible to please God" (Heb. 11:6). No matter what else you do, or how hard you try, you cannot please God if you do not believe Him.

Think about hope. The Bible says that hope produces some of the spiritual qualities that make love what it is. For example, hope produces *purity*. "And everyone who has this hope in Him purifies himself, just as He is pure" (1 John 3:3).

Hope also produces *patience*. "But if we hope for what we do not see, then we eagerly wait for it with perseverance" (Rom. 8:25).

Finally, hope produces *peace*. "This hope we have as an anchor of the soul, both sure and steadfast, and which enters the Presence behind the veil" (Heb. 6:19).

Love is still the greatest, because it is the only thing that is going to last for all eternity. When we get to heaven faith will become sight, hope will become reality, but love will still be love.

> "Faith will vanish into
>   sight;
> Hope will be emptied in
>   delight;
> But love in heaven will
>   shine more bright."

Solomon said, "Many waters cannot quench love, nor can the floods drown it" (Song of Solomon 8:7). The flood tides of time and the waves of eternity will never be able to wash love from the shores of heaven.

It was not faith that sent Jesus to die for your sins. It was not hope that sent Jesus to the cross. The only reason that God sent His Son, and the only reason His Son gave His life, was love.

That is what the world needs now, the love of God. The Bible does not say that the greatest commandment is to trust in the Lord your God. The Bible does not say that the greatest commandment is to hope in the Lord your God. The Bible says the greatest commandment is to love the Lord your God (Matt. 22:36-37). What the world eeds now is a love from God that it can give back to God, so that it can spend eternity with Him.

You need this same love; it is God's ultimate prescription. It is a love on which you can never overdose. This love which is "poured out in our hearts by the Holy Spirit" (Rom. 5:5) is the ultimate witness of a healthy, holy, and happy Christianity. "Pursue love" (1 Cor. 14:1).